CAREER IMAGING

PRINTED IN THE UNITED STATES OF AMERICA
BY
ICAN PRESS BOOK PUBLISHERS
616 THIRD AVENUE
CHULA VISTA, CA 91910

CAREER IMAGING

*HOW TO CHANGE YOUR JOB
FOR A BETTER QUALITY OF LIFE*

by

WARREN B. "DAHK" KNOX, *Ph.D., Ed.D.*

and

JANET E. KNOX, *Ph.D.*

San Diego, California
June 1993
Second Edition

ST. PHILIP'S COLLEGE LIBRARY

DISCLAIMER

All the materials in this document are either original works, contributed articles, common information shared with, by and/or for the public and its consumption; most data used is generic in nature or has come from counselors, consultants, organizations, and trainers who work or practice in Southern California. Any reproductions or contributions which are similar to or may paraphrase the works of other professionals is purely coincidental and/or accidental. The authors have, in no way, attempted to use any materials which are not of their own origination.

Printed in the United States of America
Library of Congress
Library of Congress Cataloging-in-Publication Data
ISBN # 1-88-1116-08-5
Copyright March ©1992 by Drs. W.B. and J.E. Knox

ALL RIGHTS RESERVED SECOND EDITION

All rights reserved. This material including films and tapes are solely the property of Drs. W.B. and J.E. Knox. Any resale or use in connection with a tuition, admission or like fee is strictly prohibited without the written permission of Drs. W.B. and J.E. Knox. This material including films and tapes may not be reproduced or transmitted in any form by, any means, electronic or mechanical, including photocopy recording or by any information and retrieval system without the written consent of Drs. W.B. and J.E. Knox.

ACKNOWLEDGEMENTS

The authors would like to give their thanks to all of their personal friends and relatives who have been supportive of their research and writing efforts.

Also thanks to all other professional friends, colleagues and supporters who have contributed toward the authors' endeavors to find and document answers.

Special thanks to our clients, who were the real catalysts for our deciding to write this text. This book will help other vocational counselors, career consultants, professional growth trainers, and occupational instructors, and will give some new direction and ideas for counseling clients seeking a career change.

Without the extra efforts of Patti Godsoe, Dennis Lucarelli and Josette Rice, the completion of this manuscript would have taken much longer.

"Commit to the Lord whatever you do, and your plans will succeed." (Proverbs 16:3)

Jan and Dahk Knox

> **Courage is the power to change and learn when all you can see is the difficulty of what has to be done.**
> *Jan Knox*

ICAN Press

Publisher
Dahk Knox—*Editor in Chief*

Editorial Department
Josette Rice—*Senior Editor*
Dennis Lucarelli—*Editor*
Toni Weir—*Copy Editor*
Mary Mahoney—*Copy Editor*
Jan Knox—*Staff Writer*

Art Department
Mary Weldy—*Art Director*
Susannah Myers—*Freelance Illustrator*

Typesetting
Steven Fellwock—*MIS Director*
Patricia Godsoe—*Senior Typesetter*
Sheila Williams—*Typesetter*
Wendy Weldy—*Typesetter*

Marketing
John Reid—*Marketing Director*
Dave Carroll—*Overseas Marketing Director*

Administration
Marian Denson—*Support Services Director*
Pat Redmond—*Programs Director*
Vicki Graf—*Grants Manager*
Robert Hernandez—*Administrative Assistant*
Lonnie Lewis—*Administrative Assistant*
Debbie Najera—*Administrative Assistant*

TABLE OF CONTENTS

FOREWORD v
INTRODUCTION 1
   Identifying Forgotten Dreams 4
   Why Do You Do What You Do? 7
   How Do You Resurrect
   Forgotten Dreams? 9

CAREER IMAGING 13
   It's Never Too Late
   To Start Over Again 21
   No Vision So No Excitement 26

ASSESSING THE FUNDAMENTALS
FROM THE BEGINNING 35
   Start With The Basics
   Of Your Career Life 35
   A Quick Self Survey 35
   Self Assessment And Evaluation
   Of Who You Are 39
   Personally Noted Reasons 40
   Identification Of Personal Points 43
   How You Look In Words 46
   List Of Personality Traits And Behaviors 48
   Reasons For Changing Your Career 50
   Your Honest Evaluation 55

LOOKING AHEAD TO THE FUTURE 91
   The Cycle Of Vocational Growth:
   Professional Growth Through Change 91

The Present State *93*
The Future State. *95*
Self-Assessment Of Present Job Or
Career Questions *96*
Idealizing Your Future State Of Affairs *107*
The Transitional State *110*
Actions Targeted For Results *110*
Action Steps For Goal Achievement *117*
Special Areas Of Concern *121*
List Your Strengths And Weaknesses *122*
Things In Your Life
That Must Be Changed *124*
Things You Must Be Willing To Give Up *126*
Personal Costs If You Transition *130*
Personal Costs If You Don't Do Anything *131*
Looking Ahead *133*
My List Of Future Benefits For
Making A Career Change *134*
Expected End Results *135*

THE PERSONAL PROFILE PLAN *137*
Using The Personal Profile Plan *137*
How Do I Use The Plan? *137*
The Personal Profile Plan:
A Vocational Pathway *147*
The Plan: An Outline For Successful
Job Change *149*
Lessons Learned From Your
Career/Job Change Process *176*
New Future Career Goals *178*

BIBLIOGRAPHY *179*

FOREWORD

I was flattered when asked to write the foreword for *Career Imaging*. In the past fourteen years as a vocational rehabilitation counselor I have experienced firsthand the principles set forth in this book. They really work for most people.

Should you read *Career Imaging* and perform the exercises recommended, you will be able to identify your values and define your goals and how to achieve them. Dahk and Jan Knox have presented a series of motivational career concepts in a casual, readable style, which cover a great deal of current vocational development knowledge. I personally support their emphasis on creating an image of your ideal job; this has been a technique that helped me and I recommend it to you.

Today's competitive economy requires each of us to make full use of our potential. I am confident that *Career Imaging* will contribute to your prosperity.

> Preston Chipps
> Rehabilitation Counselor

INTRODUCTION

Chances are if you're reading this book, you're not that happy or thrilled with your present job, position, or career. The choice of words you use for "job" is solely yours. We call our jobs "fun." Sure, we have our careers and we may be called the Chief Executive Officer or Editor in Chief, but our job is not work, nor is it a "job-job," it is "fun." We love it. And believe it or not, you should love what you're doing as well. If you're not, then you know why we wrote this book. And it's a good thing you bought it; now read it! It should stimulate some thinking about why you're doing what you're doing and, perhaps, convince you to try something else, something you really want to do.

People don't usually buy books like this unless they have a special need or a personal interest in the subject. Ask yourself, why did you buy this book? If you haven't bought it yet and are simply flipping through its pages and considering purchasing it, we strongly urge you to do so. But if you've already bought the book, why did you buy it?

Hopefully your reason or reasons are because you want to do something with your life that entails making a significant career change. Let's forget about the words "job" and "work," because if you bother to look them up in a thesaurus you'll find that "job" is seen as a "duty, task, assignment or discipline," among other words. "Work" is similarly equated to "labor, toil, chore, drudgery, grind, slavery, sweat, tedium and travail."

We sincerely hope you felt what we experienced while reading through those horrible little words that imply boredom, disinterest, severe mental agony and an overall yuckiness, and made us want to avoid thinking about them for another second. They are harsh and strict sounding words. When we think of "work" or "job," we think of less than positive experiences which immediately conjure up remembrances of forced behaviors and stilted conduct.

However, the word "career" is much more appealing. It mystically tells you that you are in control of your vocational destiny, if you want to be. In giving you a sense of focus and direction, it connotes an air of dimension and importance. It allows you to envision believable goals that outline your growth and development. The word "career" gives significance to your life by more adequately defining what you do as a professional vocation. . .a career. **Remember: *your career should be a labor of love, not a love (more like a hate) of labor*.**

So, let's dispense with the words "job" and "work" as they relate to your vocation or career.

What should your career be? How do you decide what career you want to pursue? Who determines the correct pathway for you to take in choosing your career? Where do you get the answers? Let's get basic. Not for long, but for just a little while. When you bake a pie, a real pie, not some instant box recipe, you have to start with the basics and progress forward. That's what's necessary for you to do with your career as well. You must begin with the fundamentals: your rudimentary interests, values and aptitudes. Why kid yourself into being something you don't really want to be? Apart from having to do some kinds of menial work or labor in order to eat and pay bills, you don't have to do anything you don't want to do. If you do perform minimum pay work, it's because you're allowing external sources, like people, things or events, to rule your life; in fact, you've personally chosen to work for pennies on the dollar.

You're responsible and you're accountable for your life. Don't blame your predicament on someone else. That's a cop out Bucko! Excuses don't fly in the real world, so if you want to be part of it, learn the rules and start being responsible and accountable for yourself. However, external influences do force you to do many things which you normally wouldn't do. The major reason for such influence is that someone wants you to become responsible and productive. Why? So you can fit the normal standards of society by conforming to the unspoken rules.

By now you're probably thinking what the devil are these folks talking about and where is all this babble leading. It's leading to you realizing some simple facts about yourself which probably haven't been super-imposed upon you by some outside influence other than your own desires. It has to do with you waking up and taking charge of your own life without interference from others who keep prodding you to conform and become another average person on the street. Mediocrity is out. There's no room for it in a successful person's life. Here's what the authors want to do: get you in touch with the possibilities of being what you want to be and properly preparing to reach, attain and maintain those personal and professional goals. The possibilities we speak of have nothing to do with Master Card or Visa, they have to do with your personal choices of a successful vocation or career. The method we've chosen, through which this is possible, is called, "finding career happiness by resurrecting your forgotten dreams."

> **Dreams can come true, they can happen to you, if you plan!**
> *Dahk Knox*

Identifying Forgotten Dreams

What are forgotten dreams? Some people don't even know they have any forgotten dreams, so it's oftentimes extremely difficult to make folks dig deep into their past to search for them. Other individuals have been quietly sitting on their forgotten dreams for years. They're right under the cushion of their chair. Oh yes, they're not forgotten either, such treasured dreams are only tucked away under that cushion for fear they might surface and have to be dealt with, the shame of it all!

So, what are those dreams? They are everybody's secret desires, wants, likes, whims, fancies, notions, ambitions, aspirations, hungers, hankerings, cravings, musings, visions and fantasies. They are the suppressed needs you've never been able to fulfill, the latent "core" challenges, thirsts and yearnings which you've skated around for years, maybe decades. They *ARE* your most passionate creative remonstrations of expression which have been expostulating and protesting their confinement while simultaneously making you the incomplete person you've become.

However, forgotten dreams are really not forgotten and they've never gone away; leastwise, not very far. They've only locked themselves into the shallowest recesses of your mind. For some of you they've been superficial itches which you couldn't scratch, perennial pains that wouldn't go away and leave you alone, or headaches that have come and gone with your rising or declining worries of work.

Anxiety and fear often accompany such dreams. Why? Because most people who want more out of life continue to suppress their forgotten dreams by trying to force them further into the black holes of their minds. It never ceases to amaze the authors, but most people instead of encouraging their dreams to surface, fail to recognize what they have to offer. People have a terrible tendency to avoid those ascending possibilities and stifle them with excuses and denials. It's the old *Negative Success Factor: people want to be successful but they don't want to be the progenitors of their own success for fear of failure or ridicule*. Why?

Because failure is directly attributable to themselves. Oh, God, spare them the embarrassment!

It's time to start finding your own career happiness by resurrecting those forgotten dreams. You need to take the initiative and force yourself, if necessary, to meet the personal challenges you've always wanted to face but didn't because of other influences. It's never too late to start identifying and developing those dreams, those desires, those creative urges which silently scream for your proactive approval and action. Don't just sit there after you read this book, get up and do something! This is your life and it only goes around one time, unless you want to risk reincarnation. . .and that's no sure bet. The only thing holding you back is yourself, is yourself, is yourself, is . . .

> **Set before yourself a great and definite life purpose. Hidden away in your innermost soul is a transcendent ideal capable of realization. What you need is not more capacity or greater opportunity, but increased resolution and concentration. Nothing will give you so much pleasure as the consciousness of making daily progress toward a great life purpose.**
> *Grenville Kleisen*

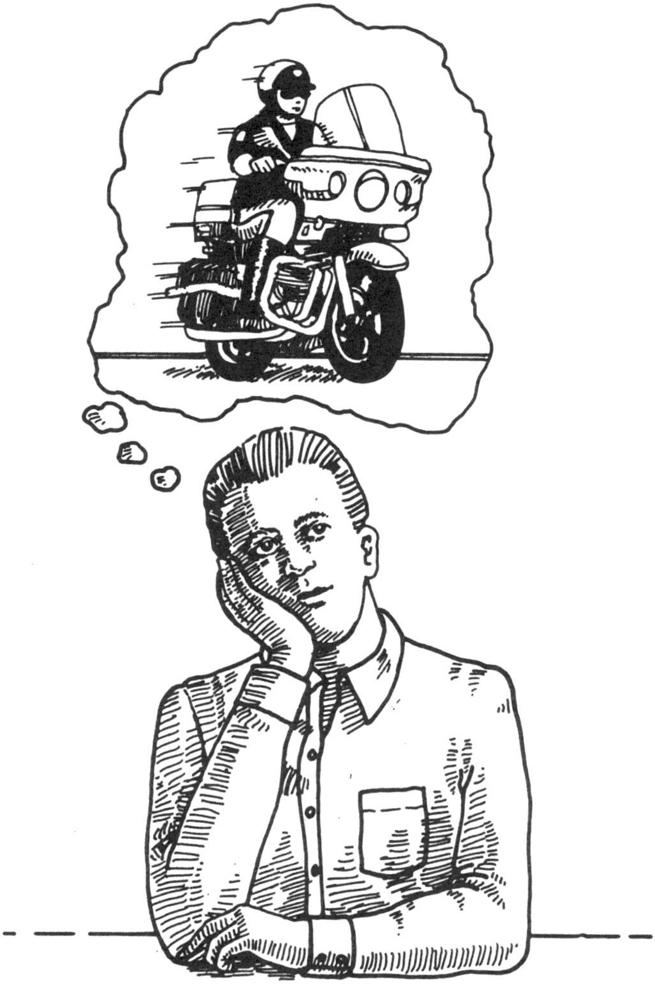

NOTES

Why Do You Do What You Do?

After reading everything which preceded this portion of the text, do you understand what the authors are getting at? Have you begun to grasp the gravity of your own stilted situation? Do you fall into the group of people who haven't the foggiest notion as to why they do the things they do, other than that someone else said it was probably best for them? Is it best for you? Why? If you are truly reading this book seriously, purchased it with your hard earned money, and said "yes" to that last question, you need help. Get real! Do it fast!

Are you part of the group that gets up each morning, or evening, depending on your shift, and goes to work to make money to pay the bills and feed the family, among other secondary reasons? Have you bothered to think about why you behave as such? Is it because you needed the money to survive and the job you have is the only job you could get, or were offered? Do you continue to labor at your position without having an end goal which daily lights up your life and gets you excited about working?

Why do you do what you do? What are your excuses for not being you and having fun with your career? Could it be that it really isn't a career at all, but only a job? And how long will you continue to let that job be your "downer" career? Bubba, there's no substitute for the real thing! Quit lying to yourself and vacuum the sand out of your ears. You'll drown in your own inner ocean of avoidance and unawareness, choked by itsy-bitsy ripples of stagnant, deplorable passivity. It's too bad, because you could be riding the Banzai Pipeline of investigative curiosity and creativity. You should be preparing for something better than that "samo-samo" boring and relentless job, late night TV, a six pack of beer, or a bowl of ice cream, reruns of Hard Copy and Matlock, cutting the wet lawn early on Saturday then shoving off for the desert in your affordable mid-sized import so you can dune-buggy and drink more beer on Sunday. Ask yourself this question, "Is my life really that disgusting?"

> **To have a great purpose to work for, a purpose larger than ourselves, is one of the secrets of making life significant. Successful careers are motivated by great desires.**
> *Alfred Armand Montapert*

So Bubba, what's your purpose? Let us run that by you one more time. What's your purpose? Why are you here on Earth? To do what we just outlined above? We certainly hope not, but if the profile fits, then it's time you started to do something to change all that nonsense and turn your unproductive time into enthusiastic plans for real accomplishment. When you understand the purpose for your being (and we are speaking about your career, your professional being, not the mysteries of life and the universe) then you'll start to glean the importance of what you could be doing and what you would have to contribute to yourself and society as a whole. Total up your parts. The axiom goes something like: the sum of the parts is equal to the total of the whole, rabbits multiply quicker when the tides rise, and once a BMW owner, always a BMW owner. You get the gist. We surmise you're quick, right?

How Do You Resurrect Forgotten Dreams?

Start considering a schedule for resurrecting those forgotten dreams. Second thought, hold the first thought. Resurrect those forgotten dreams while you're still hot on the notion, it's for your own benefit. How do you do that, you say? It's rather easy as the content goes, it's the bloody process which causes so many mini-agonies. Follow our method very closely and don't deviate from its direction.

In Dr. John L. Holland's book, *Making Vocational Choices*, he speaks of a revised theory of careers and their applications to vocational life. His theory of careers is used to explain universal and generic career phenomena, report new vocational gleanings and their supportive research data, and to identify those concepts for career and vocational assistance and counseling. Dr. Holland's theory intersects with many of the authors' own principles, assumptions, presumptions and suppositions.

One of our suppositions similar to that of Dr. Holland's work is that there are certain basic questions which need to be asked, for data gathering purposes, in order to fully explain vocational behaviors which affect career changes. Those questions are:

(1) What are the most effective methods for providing vocational counseling to folks with professional/occupational problems?

(2) What personal, professional, social, and environmental factors result in non-achievement, under-achievement, career indecisiveness, disappointment from incorrect or bad judgments, or a significant lack of accomplishment?

(3) What personal, professional, social and environmental factors result in achievement, accomplishment and career decisiveness?

(4) What personal, professional, social and environmental factors determine the balance, adjustments, and/or transitions of a person's chosen occupation and their level of responsibility?

(5) What are the most beneficial and effective methods of evaluating, assessing and measuring successful performance as a result of vocational counseling?

In order to properly implement the process of resurrecting your forgotten dreams, the wise and astute vocational counselor will take into consideration the five questions above and assure himself or herself that he or she has all the answers necessary to project a pathway for success. Acting on the answers is up to you. Having answered the above questions to the liking of the vocational counselor and yourself, together you begin to explore the responses and develop or plan an orderly career transition. **However, you can begin the roadwork without the counselor, in the peaceful surroundings of your own home, or some other quiet place.** That roadwork consists of your personal inputs listed on paper, for later reference and review, which depict your innermost career desires and occupational wishes.

> **A dream is the first step in the beginning of your new career.**
> *Jan Knox*

When you close your eyes you can focus your thoughts on some other place, in some other setting, doing something totally different from what you are doing or are used to doing. The point here is to create an ideal picture of what you'd like to be doing and where you'd like to be doing it. For this part of the process you don't need the vocational counselor, only your own wild imagination. But please be serious! This process is labeled *"Career Imaging."*

**Jot Down Your Dreams.
Use Your Imagination.**

CAREER IMAGING

Step One: Find a nice quiet place where you won't be disturbed by others. Do not play any music, not even for creating a false mood. This activity isn't a meditation process, it's solely for stimulating your mental resources by concentrating on images which project visual pictures or representations of "you" engaged in an activity which you greatly desire.

Step Two: Find a comfortable spot to sit, or perhaps you prefer to lie down. Just get comfortable so you can concentrate on the images you're after without being hampered by physical discomfort or displeasure. If you have some external stimulus bothering you, it'll be imperative for you to eliminate that problem. You won't be able to achieve the results you want, if you're concerned with other things going on around you; especially if such external influences are interfering with your ability to focus and concentrate.

Step Three: Clear your mind of thoughts and ideas which may be cluttering its ability to centralize and accentuate the core images which you are hopeful of shaping. If you're going through a stressful period of time in your life, or even if your day has been especially traumatic, for one reason or another, then this isn't the time to be spending on your "career imaging." Wait for the right time, when you don't have anything hanging over your head. When you feel free of emotional stress and pressure from unfinished business or personal/professional problems. *You won't be effective with this step if you aren't free of mental problems.* Trying to concentrate on mental career images will be like trying to silently pray when you keep getting side tracked or continue to doze off into dreamland.

Step Four: Once you've established your comfort zone, cleared your mind and are free of outside influences and noises, you'll be ready to mentally begin and commit to your thinking process; that is, you'll be ready for career imaging. Start by relaxing and breathing regularly. Don't breathe too shallowly but don't breathe too deeply either. **The focus of your concentration is going to be on potential idyllic career possibilities**, not on meditation and fanciful visions of floating on clouds or sailing peacefully over the ocean. Center your thoughts on "productive activity" which pictures you doing something significant that equates to self-satisfaction.

Note carefully what it is you're doing and where you're performing this activity. What you do and where you do it are essential in eventually establishing your own acceptable measure of involvement and believability. Although this is intangible, it is also concrete perceptible evidence. How can that be? Because your thoughts are real in themselves. They may exist only in invisible pictures, but nevertheless, they have real substance because your mind brought them into being. They'll stay with you throughout your life, as long as you have sufficient interest and curiosity. Work with those invisible pictures and you could create a new and exciting career for yourself. You have to give them a chance. Something inside your psyche has stimulated their existence. That means they are valuable thoughts to you, thoughts which you have turned into vocational ideas. Try developing them further. They're yours, exclusively yours.

For instance: You see yourself on the beaches of Cabo San Lucas, in Mexico. You're not actually working, but you're engaged in some form of water activity. You flash from surfing, to parasailing, to wind surfing, to boogie-boarding, to being back again on the beach and simply watching yourself having fun. That's a very important word, *fun*. There isn't any reason why you shouldn't be having fun at what you're doing. *Fun is not only paramount but is the instrumental central core of becoming totally enmeshed and successful at what you'll eventually be doing with your life*.

So there you are on a beautiful beach in Cabo San Lucas. We've already determined the location and the variety of activities that have captured your attention. Now, how are you going to sift through the activities and figure out what it all means? Does this mental picture simply mean you're fantasizing about taking a vacation to some sunny, exotic spot in Southern Baja Mexico, or does it mean something more important? You have to be the one who determines the significance of your own mental image. However, if the thought of you just being there on vacation keeps creeping into your mind, then perhaps you only see this image as an escape from reality, or a place to go on some future vacation.

On the other hand, where you are and what you're doing in that dream could mean something more exciting than just a one or two week vacation. It could mean you should consider seeking a profession which allows you to do and be in the midst of the things you love. This could connote the possibility of you becoming interested in handling tourist recreational activities for some resort. Sure! Why not? If that's what you want, why not? If you think it's only a fanciful notion, then that's exactly what it will become, a crazy, wild fanciful notion. But if you seriously consider the reality of going to Mexico, or some place similar in the United States, and becoming a recreational director, *you can make it happen*. Only your thinking will make it possible or impossible.

Forget money and expenses for the moment. Simply concentrate on the possibility of following your dream. Your first career image has cast you a heavy load, it says you want to be on the beach enjoying life and working at the same time. Working, such an ugly word, working, yuk! Use some other word, like "engaged" or "involved." Such words take the edge off the whole process of "doing what you like to do." If you decide you'll do something proactive which leads you toward achieving your mental goal of becoming an activity director for some resort, then we guarantee that your possibility of reaching your eventual goal is very good. If, however, you never get out of the dream but glue your feet firmly back on the ground, you'll continue doing what you have been doing, and you'll probably never look back. The shame of it all. You had the goal/dream in sight, but for fear of reality you let it go and with it went your hopes of a better tomorrow. With it went your "career imaging" ideal job and with that was buried another dream, a soon to be forgotten dream. At present, your unachieved career happiness will once again be neglected and you'll continue to calcify in your current rut. So don't belly ache, you had the chance to change your life for the better, but you failed to believe in your own ability and potential.

A few of you will go for the gusto. You'll decide to make a positive change in your life and you'll begin to plan how to make the necessary changes so you can prepare to become an activity director for that exotic resort. Those folks who go after that dream will most likely succeed; all they need is a good plan to make it happen. Part of that plan involves the money and expenses we told you to forget a few paragraphs ago. Now it's time to factor them into your plan.

If you think you can just quit your profession and start going after your dream immediately, you're in for a rather rude awakening. Unless you have saved beaucoup bucks to cover this up-coming change in your career, you will probably fail financially. So there is a practical and economical side to this change. Although your career imaging didn't make you aware of such a necessity, remember, you created those pictures by forming your conscious thoughts into pleasurable images.

> **I respect the man who knows what he wishes. The greatest part of all the mischief in the world arises from the fact that men do not sufficiently understand their own aims. They have undertaken to build a tower, and spend no more labor on the foundation than would be necessary to erect a hut.**
> *Johann W. von Goethe*

When was the last time you had a pleasurable image about "financial and economic stability" that didn't originally stem from your grounded sense of reality? To put it more plainly, your career imaging process will usually produce the desired possibilities you'd love to do, but the grounded sense of reality which possesses you is focused on the "here and now" and demands unrestricted accountability and responsible behavior.

That last statement is not a catch-22, it's simply a balanced look at the difference between "what can be" and "what is." What you have to do to achieve the "what can be" status of your future is to find the happy medium between the career imaging dream and the reality of the present. To do this means you'll have to sit down and carefully plan your transition from accountant, banker, computer operator, cashier, or some other profession to that of becoming a recreational activity director at some exotic resort. This isn't all fanciful, it's possible.

If you think it's not, just call long distance to The Cliffs timeshare condominiums in Princeville, Kauai; or to Sandals or Couples Resort in Ocho Rios or Montego Bay, Jamaica and ask to speak with the current Activities Director. Ask him or her what they did to get to where they are, doing what they are doing, and do they still like it. Now remember, if you want to be an activity director in some nice place like Jamaica or Kauai, you probably won't be getting rich. To become independently wealthy, you'll have to have your own business or become the big boss, then you'll realize increased salary or profits. But simply being an employee will not guarantee you riches. However, will you achieve becoming what you wanted to become?

Part of the transition process from "what you are now" to "what you'll become" is knowing "what to expect" from "what you do." Check out all the angles involved in changing from one career to another. Hang in there, because later in this book, we're going to give you a plan, a personal pathway which will assist you in making your career change.

> **What I need is somebody to make me do what I can.**
> *Ralph Waldo Emerson*

Also, keep in mind we've chosen only one career imaging profession to illustrate how you can make your favorite dreams become a real possibility. It may be you were dreaming about becoming an entrepreneur in the fashion merchandising industry; or perhaps you saw yourself involved in some other capacity which requires different parameters or sets of circumstances than just being on the beach with a group of tourists. You get to choose your own example; you're the captain of your dreams so steer a straight course toward your desired goal. Sometimes the freedom of choice is exhilarating. But sometimes its a curse and can be extremely frustrating. Like we said, the choice is all yours, so choose wisely.

Step Five: Once you've completed your career imaging and have chosen one, two or even three potential new areas of interest, you must become involved in researching the possibilities of making those spotlighted desires become realities. This particular step is very involved in that it demands a considerable amount of your personal time. You cannot just turn a dream into a reality by wishing it so and doing little or nothing else to secure its birth. However, you can make that dream become a reality by preparing for its birth and nurturing it along, step by step. Therefore, the involvement on your part is extensive. But ask yourself, how badly do I want this to happen? And, what am I willing to do to make it so? How committed are you to changing your life and becoming the person you've always wanted to be and possibly never knew or realized? Yes, perhaps you've been someone else locked up in your mind, struggling to get out and blossom? The time is close at hand, go for it!

To be very sure, *Step Five* must start with a commitment for change and a conviction you'll see it through to the end. If you aren't committed to making a change in your career, or if you don't hold certain convictions how you'll succeed and achieve desired results, then don't try to make your dreams become realities. Stay uninvolved and unfulfilled. Continue to be not quite as happy as you really could be and see how satisfied you'll be with yourself several years down the road when you're kicking yourself in the fanny and saying, "I wish I'd done that!"

> **"Can't" never could 'til he tried!**

It's Never Too Late To Start Over Again

One of the biggest excuses we hear, concerning starting over again, is "It's too late for me. Look how old I am, I don't have the time; I should be getting ready for retirement." Listen Bucko, *when you quit laughing and learning, you quit living*. And as the saying goes, "that's the name of that tune." Thank you Robert Blake. Quit making excuses for yourself. If you can't stay open-minded with the hope of a second or third career, then you haven't got a chance in Hell of being successful at one. So, you might as well buy right into your excuse. Or any other excuse will work just as well. Which one works for you? If it's really original, please mail it to our publisher, the address is inside the book. We'll be happy to review your excuse, rate it for its originality and possibly use it in a new book called, "Why Things Never Work For Me," or, "Oh My God, I've Run Out Of Time!"

If you're searching for your first career, chances are very good you'll find at least one or two good areas of interest and "turn-on." The excitement of having that happen to you is wonderful. It brightens up your overall outlook on life and makes each day a pleasure to get up and go for the gold all day.

Those of you who are dilly dallying around, trying yet not trying too hard, to make up your mind and decide whether early retirement is best or not, you have got to make some positive, concrete decisions. Don't be a dud. There's too much action in life to settle for a twilight existence of slumber, suds and solace. Consider what you have to contribute and put back into life. Yes, if life was good to you and you have special skills, then start sharing those skills with others who need to develop them and improve their own lot. At least be useful and productive. Who ever said retirement had to be a life of gradual attrition and decline, or continual slow lateral movement.

Sharing those skills just may be your ticket to teaching or instruction. Perhaps you'll only be able to mentor one or two people, but at least you're doing something useful to someone else. And it's appreciated by those who receive your assistance. Let's face it, personal accomplishment is never dull, nor is it unrewarding.

We aren't trying to tell you to become a teacher or an instructor, but if the shoe fits then go for it! The point is, do something with the rest of your life instead of sitting on the couch and watching television. You'll live longer if you do. *You must stay active and involved.* Think of all the things you've always wanted to do, take some positive action, and gradually work yourself into a committed frame of mind to do something new and exciting. Quit vegging!

Ask yourself why you didn't do any of the things you always wanted to do. Ask yourself why you can't do them now. And when you start giving yourself dozens of excuses, that's when you know you've succumbed to laziness and are headed for an early grave. We guarantee you'll live longer (if you are physically and mentally healthy) when you become totally enmeshed in something worthwhile and productive. If you decide to keep vegging, at least send us those great excuses.

Get interested and excited, but most of all, get real! Throw your lousy excuses out the window, they're not worth the time you spent considering them. Target a simple goal and focus on the positive aspects of how you can go about accomplishing your expected results. *It's never too late to start a second or third career, but thinking makes it so.*

> **Things move so fast today that we sometimes get the feeling our solutions may be obsolete before we can get them worked out.**
> *Bits And Pieces, August 1989*

So get your head screwed on right, and tight, and start making things happen for yourself. There's nothing worse than someone who is whiny and fastened to their pity-pot, sulking and finding reasons why they can't do something. If that's the profile you paint for yourself, then you've ignorantly and inadvertently planned some real rough roads ahead. However, no road is so long that you can't reach it's end. Change your tears and fears to cheers and gears, wind up and happily get going. All you need is a good Hank Williams Jr. "attitude adjustment."

You folks who are older and have retired, consider all of the famous people who started second careers and became well known for their twilight achievements and contributions to mankind. Many such individuals got to use their special skills for the first time in their lives. Why did they wait so long? Because they were locked into traditional ways of thinking; they had stilted beliefs about how they could only perform one kind of task and were further convinced, by societal beliefs, how they should hold on to that job they'd already worked at for years. Why? Because of financial security, or like we've already said, "traditional stigma," and nothing else.

Such thinking most always leads to a lack-luster life without excitement and real fulfillment. Get going and start doing the things you've always wanted to do. Start NOW!

> **Success or failure is caused more by our "mental attitudes" than by our "mental capacities." The accurate thinker examines the sources of his formation, weighs statements for motivations, and tests their reasonableness.**
> *Alfred Armand Montapert*

> **People keep asking me when I'm going to retire. They say you're supposed to slow down and take it easy when you get old... If I had started slowing down when I was 65 or 70, by now I'd be stopped. A turtle would move faster. But I didn't slow down, I kept going. And now there isn't a turtle around that can pass me.**
> *George Burns*

> There is only one thing which will really train the human mind and that is the voluntary use of the mind by the man himself. You may aid him, you may guide him, you may suggest to him, and above all you may inspire him; but the only thing worth having is that which he gets by his own exertions; and what he gets is proportionate to the effort he puts into it.
> *A. Lawrence Lowell*

No Vision So No Excitement

Last year we watched a television program called, "Street Stories," hosted by Ed Bradley of "60 Minutes." It was not only unbelievable what we heard some individuals say, it was inconceivable how any person with an active brain and a healthy body would've said what they did. What did they say? Here's the scenario, it's one of having no vision, having become "brain dead" toward finding a suitable or better alternative.

> **Winners never quit and quitters never win!**

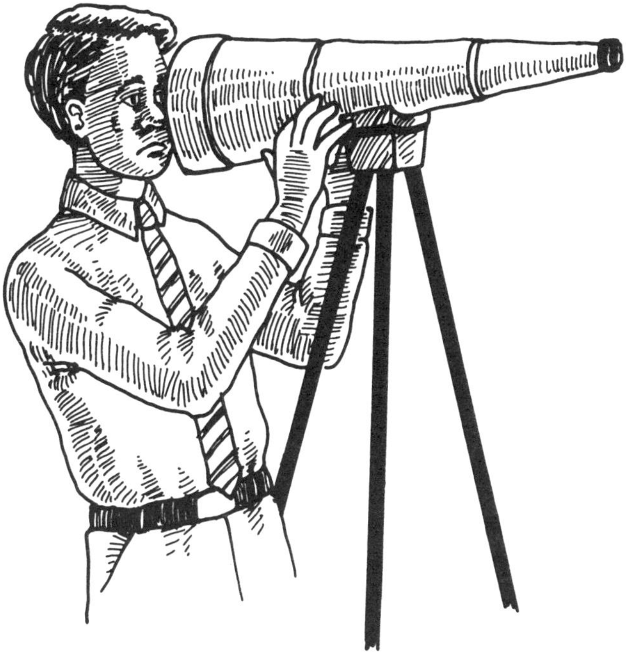

NOTES

There's absolutely nothing wrong with making your living from using your hands. For centuries people have forged out a living from doing the best they can, under all kinds of circumstances and conditions, with sometimes only basic tools. No matter what it was they did, if they worked hard enough and focused their resources on their tasks, they were able to succeed and bring home the bacon. They did this by working with their hands.

We've all heard the terms "blue collar" and "white collar." These terms denote a certain class of job. Don't worry about our choice of word, "class," because it's unavoidable, "blue collar" and "white collar" are classes. They are classes of work, and those classes of work accordingly produce their own specific class of people. Or people become products of their class of work. Forget the semantics, the choice is yours.

Most blue collar workers are on the lower end of the wage earning scale and often realize fewer benefits than their counterparts on the higher end of the wage scale, the white collar workers. Yet there are some blue collar manufacturing and industrial jobs that pay very well and offer excellent benefits, while there are white collar positions that blatantly discriminate by paying awful wages for what the job requires. Certain parts of the United States have an abundance of certain types of workers. If the abundance is high, then the choices of the employers is much greater. Therefore, they can pay lower wages and get exceptionally higher qualified people for peanuts.

Example: Southern California probably has one of the higher concentrations of educated individuals in the country. There are more folks with Masters degrees and PhDs out of work, or working at menial jobs than you can imagine. And that Bucko, is a fact. Weekly we encounter numerous individuals, over-educated and over-qualified, as the employers so coldly label them, coming to see us, or calling us for job search assistance, training and placement. Their biggest gripe is not being able to find suitable employment for their skills, competencies, knowledge and prior accumulated work experience.

As a matter of fact, most of these people have to work at jobs far below their abilities and aptitudes; that is, if they have been lucky enough to find a job. Notice: we are not saying anything here about careers, we are talking basic "pay the bills" jobs. That's exactly what happens when the job market is in a terrible slump. We call it a recession when there aren't adequate positions available for individuals who have the education to excel and get ahead.

In a similar way, certain areas of the country offer low paying jobs to blue collar workers because they have an abundance of them to select from as well. For instance, along the Mexican borders of the United States, what occurs as concerns industry? You've got it, cheap labor. Who takes advantage of it? Big manufacturing industries in particular. Why should some Japanese television manufacturer set up shop in San Diego and have to pay minimum wages to American blue collar workers, when they can go into Tijuana and hire Mexican workers to do the same jobs for pennies on the dollar?

> **People keep yelling,
> "Buy American, buy American."
> But then they themselves go out
> and buy Japanese and try to justify their
> purchases by saying, "Well, it may be a
> Japanese company, but it's 70% made in
> Tennessee by American workers."**
> *More Than One Person*

You tell us, who suffers? Obviously this is a good thing for the economy of Mexico, and God knows they need it desperately, but what about American workers? How many American workers were out of jobs when their company pulled up roots and moved to some new location which enables them to operate cheaper and more economically? You see the picture, everyone sees the picture; there's no mystery in what is happening and it will continue to escalate.

The authors aren't offering an answer to this problem, we're only shedding light upon it because it's an unfortunate example of American workers losing their jobs for all the wrong humane reasons. Why? So big industry can survive and make MORE PROFIT. Profit isn't a dirty word, but when you go after it at the expense of someone else's livelihood, it sure as hell is! And that's what is going on, and we, the country as a whole, continue to allow it to happen. This is a good example of how external influences affect personal lives. Please, close your eyes and pin the tail on the donkey!

> **Each problem has hidden in it an opportunity so powerful that it literally dwarfs the problem. The greatest success stories were created by people who recognized a problem and turned it into an opportunity.**
> *Joseph Sugarman*

However, what about the "Street Stories" scenario? We haven't forgotten, we just needed to lay a little ground work around the concept of blue collar/white collar jobs. Let's look at what occurred on this television show. You should find this interesting, it should make you begin to think and perhaps, thank your own lucky stars for giving you insight to the alternatives that life offers you.

> **The golden opportunity you are seeking is in yourself. It is not in your environment; it is not in luck or chance, or the help of others; it is in yourself alone.**
> *Orison Swett Marden*

Somewhere in Indiana a small steel company went under, after a century of successful operation, and had to lay off all its employees. Many of the men who were employed at the mill knew nothing beyond the steel industry and the life it provided for their families. To be exact, these men knew only how to perform their own specific jobs. Those jobs called for exceptional manual labor and a specific knowledge of their well honed expertise in making tools out of the molten metal.

After the lay off, Ed Bradley visited the town and interviewed some of the workers who were laid off. What is interesting although tragic, is the attitude of the majority of the workers. After considerable time off, most hadn't found alternative work. And being versed in the steel industry and knowing little about any other type of work, these folks may stay unemployed without getting new training.

Here is an example of the attitude, and this is what the authors are especially concerned about, the workers total surrender and capitulation to their undeserved fate and the complete absence of work/career alternatives. In other words, there was an utter lack of vision for other options.

When one plant manager was interviewed concerning the steel industry, he showed how most the work would now be performed by computers. Therefore, the old jobs which took a certain amount of skilled labor and expertise had become archaic over night; this would force the workers who were laid off to go get new training which offered the skill level necessary to handle the computerized tasks. We didn't hear one laid off worker mention how he would seek and obtain such training. Not one!

Two things did happen however. One, a gentleman who was laid off sold his home and everything he had and purchased a World War I machine which allowed him to open up his own small steel business and employ a few of his longtime comrades, but he couldn't hire everybody. Many of those who were not hired showed up just to watch the others work. They said the steel dust was in their blood and would be impossible to get out. In essence they were saying they would never be able to do anything else but forge steel and so forth. They had no inkling of doing anything else nor were they willing to realize the potential for starting a new career.

One individual sat on his pity-pot all day and hung around his home while his wife continued to work at her job. He said, even at 36 years of age, he might as well die. He had nothing to live for, all he knew was getting up and going to work. Now that such an opportunity had been taken away from him, he considered shooting himself. How tragic! No vision!

> **Where there is no vision, the people perish.**
> *Proverbs 29:18*

Of course, you could be saying, "come on guys, get real about this situation," and simultaneously thinking, "so what other alternatives did they have?" Oh, believe us, there are always alternatives, and when you think there are none, that is when you give in and lose at life.

First, it was the workers' loss. Nobody had ever educated them to look for opportunity or work beyond the fires of the mill. They had no knowledge of what else was available to them, so they've remained ignorant of what other possibilities exist. It's no wonder they've developed tunnel vision. They've never been educated about other opportunities or training.

Fortunately for you, you've been given that opportunity and we certainly hope that's why you purchased this book, to view the possibilities life holds for you. We won't belabor the misfortunes of the steel workers any further. Their example was to show you how a class of workers, without any knowledge of options and alternatives, simply allow themselves to whither away and throw the towel of life into the ring. It's a horrible shame. Someone needs to show them a new vision. ***Remember: without a vision there's no future, nor is there excitement about one's future, or excitement about life in general***. We feel for the worker who may tragically take his own life over this loss and we hope somebody in Indiana has the insight and compassion to intervene and assist this young man and his family.

You are a fortuitous person. Why? Because you've had the insight and understanding to know there's more to life than what has already happened to you. That's why you are reading about how to discover some new ways which will assist you in changing your life for the better. That's precisely why the authors wrote this book. In the next section of this book, we'll look at some of those ideas.

> If you stand up to be counted, from time to time you may even get yourself knocked down. But remember this: someone flattened by an opponent can get up. Someone flattened by conformity stays down for good.
> *Thomas J. Watson, Jr.*

> One of life's little ironies is the fact that when you finally master a tough job you make it look easy.
> *Bits & Pieces 3/92*

ASSESSING THE FUNDAMENTALS FROM THE BEGINNING

Start With The Basics Of Your Career Life

Seriously examine what you're presently doing for work. It's obviously no longer a career for you. If you think it still is, then you may be kidding yourself into accepting fiction for fact. You wouldn't be researching career sources if you hadn't considered changing jobs. If you've been forced into this situation due to lay off, work release, being fired, long/short term unemployment, or if you've recently quit working, then those are excellent reasons to also be researching your alternatives and preparing to do something constructive. After you've finished considering leaving your present position or thinking about a career change, answer the following fundamental questions:

A Quick Self Survey

(1) Why are you and why have you been doing this job?

(2) Why are you working in this career field?

(3) Why are you working where you are and for who you are?

(4) Why are you considering leaving (not motivation but reason)?

(5) What has motivated you to consider changing jobs or careers?

(6) How soon do you want to leave your job?

(7) What plans have you made to do so?

(8) Have you already started to explore career options?

(9) Have you formed any ideas for making changes career change?

(10) Have you considered resurrecting some of those old forgotten dreams?

So, what do you think about your answers to the above questions? Are you seriously ready to do some planning and preparation for making a career change? If your answer is "yes," good for you. If it's "no," why are you dragging your booty on making a decision? This is your life, your career, your time. Why waste it? Start doing something which will produce something positive. A good start would be to conduct a self-assessment.

This is similar to answering the questions in the above survey, only you'll be focusing on some rather specific elements of your life and trying to coordinate those identifications and results with a new professional career. A personal assessment of your values, interests, work ethics and morals, abilities and aptitudes, environmental choices and work styles, skills and competencies, knowledge and education, training and work experiences, and any other area you feel is consequential, should be thoroughly examined and clarified.

If you don't assess yourself and the areas identified above, you'll probably not focus on the right elements necessary to be understood, before making that significant career change. Please listen to this advice and do things correctly. Accurate results and findings of your personal assessment may assist you in beginning to systematically recognize and distinguish your career preferences and possibilities.

> **Nurture your mind with great thoughts.**
> *Disraeli*

> **Know what you've got before you try to get going!**
> *Jan Knox*

Keep in mind, your selection of a career is most likely a representation or characterization of your personality. Your choice or choices of a career may easily be subtle extensions or expressions of your personality.

> More recent knowledge about the personal and environmental factors associated with vocational choice, job changes, and vocational achievement has revealed the need for a broader conception... just as we have developed theories of personality from our knowledge of sex and parental relationships, so we can construct theories of personality from our knowledge of vocational life. We can then reinterpret vocational interests as an expression of personality.
> — *Dr. John L. Holland*

If the choice of your career is nothing more than a personal behavior which identifies your motivations, abilities, skills, personality characteristics and traits, or your educational experiences, then what you'll be especially concerned with is finding a career which will be a way of life for you. Such an occupation should set the tenor and quality of environment in which you'll eventually desire to be part of, live in and work in, or have the freedom of self-expression without fear of ridicule, rejection or external pressures which cause pressure, stress or anxiety.

Self-Assessment And Evaluation Of Who You Are

A self-assessment and evaluation of yourself and what you were able to unearth and identify is nothing more than an examination of what you stand for, believe in, have convictions toward, hope to achieve or accomplish, and of satisfying deeds you desire to fulfill or what you want to become or do with your life. Your findings are solely based on the data you input into your self-assessment. If you don't tell the whole truth to yourself, then your results will be false. Therefore, you'll fail to construct an accurate picture of the "real you."

On the other hand, if you're honest and sincere with your answers, then you'll be able to predicate your career plans on the basis of fact and truth. This should be most desirable to you, this is your life, right? Let's reiterate what you should examine about yourself:

(1) What do you stand for?

(2) What do you believe in?

(3) What do you have strong convictions toward?

(4) What do you hope to achieve?

(5) What satisfying deeds do you desire to fulfill?

(6) What do you want to become or do with your life?

This is a simple, basic self-assessment. If you can identify at least five good concrete points for each of the above questions, then you'll have something substantial and significant with which you can begin to determine "what you are all about." Do this exercise in two parts: first make a list of five noted reasons for each of the questions already listed; secondly, write a short synopsis of those points, forming a paragraph which spells out, in plain language, what the five points mean when blended or mixed together. Let's see who you are!

Personally Noted Reasons

(1) What I Stand For:

a. _____

b. _____

c. _____

d. _____

e. _____

(2) What I Believe In:

a._____

b._____

c._____

d._____

e._____

(3) What I Have Strong Convictions Toward:

a._____

b._____

c._____

d._____

e._____

(4) What I Hope To Achieve:

a._____

b._____

c._____

d._____

e._____

(5) What Satisfying Deeds I Hope To Fulfill:

a._____

b._____

c._____

d._____

e._____

(6) What I Hope To Do With My Life:

a._____

b._____

c._____

d._____

e._____

> Self-centered individuals are those people who engage in so much idle chit-chat about themselves that nobody else gets a chance to talk about themselves, even if they really knew who they were.
> *Dahk Knox*

Identification Of Personal Points

(1) What Do You Stand For?

_____

_____

_____

_____

_____

(2) What Do You Believe In?

_____

_____

_____

_____

_____

(3) What Do You Have Strong Convictions Toward?

_____

_____

_____

_____

_____

(4) What Do You Hope To Achieve?

_____

_____

(5) What Satisfying Deed Do You Desire To Fulfill?

(6) What Do You Want To Become Or Do With Your Life?

> **Most of us learn more from our own mistakes than we do from good examples set by others.**

How You Look In Words

Now that you've had a chance to reflect on yourself and write a few concrete thoughts which, hopefully, have helped to shape your thinking about potential careers, let's move on further in the same direction. Although you've had a chance to assess some of your strongest characteristics, which make up a significant portion of your personality, take the time to look over the **List Of Personality Traits And Behaviors** and identify the words which apply to you.

The following paragraph is paraphrased from the July 1990 publication of *Bits & Pieces*. Successful people generally have three basic characteristics in addition to their technical skills. They are:

Self-esteem: People who have self-respect are very productive. They're self-assured and optimistic about the future. Such folks have an abundance of positive feelings about themselves.

Control: Effective people are in charge of their own lives. Accordingly, they accept responsibility for their failures and claim credit for their successes.

Energy: Energetic people usually become exceptionally successful in their careers. People who act, look and talk energetically will get the job done. They walk their talk. These are people whose 'will do' will measure up to their 'can do' every time.

Self-esteem, energy and control label a person as outwardly successful. Others will naturally gravitate to them.

> **Only as you know yourself can your brain serve you as a sharp and efficient tool. Know your own failings, passions, and prejudices so you can separate them from what you see.**
> *Bernard M. Baruch*

List Of Personality Traits And Behaviors

Accountable	Eager	Natural
Adaptive	Empathetic	Negotiator
Aggressive	Empowering	Nut Case
Analytical	Energetic	Organized
Assertive	Enthusiastic	Persistent
Attentive	Flexible	Persuasive
Believable	Forceful	Planner
Careful	Friendly	Poised
Communicative	Handy	Polite
Competent	Helpful	Practical
Competitive	Honest	Punctual
Concerned	Imaginative	Resourceful
Confident	Innovative	Relentless
Considerate	Knowledgeable	Resilient
Cooperative	Leader	Self-Assured
Creative	Listener	Self-Confident
Decisive	Loyal	Self-Controlled
Delegating	Managerial	Self-Disciplined
Deliberate	Maturity	Self-Starter
Dependable	Moral	Trustworthy
Dignified	Motivational	Versatile

The purpose of this exercise has been for you to take a second look at yourself in terms of words, rather than phrases. You've summed up some of your personal feelings about important opinions, emotions and beliefs, now how do you see yourself in words? Which ten words are the most significant to you? List them on the lines provided.

(1)_____ (6) _____

(2)_____ (7)_____

(3)_____ (8)_____

(4)_____ (9)_____

(5)_____ (10)_____

Why are these particular ten words more important or significant than any other ten words? Why do you think they apply more to you than some other choices? State your reasons below.

Answer:_____

_____

_____

_____

_____

_____

Reasons For Changing Your Career

How do you know for sure it's time to start considering a job or career change? Everybody has an opinion about what is the final straw, the ultimate determining factor, the absolute threshold of endurance, the moment of truth, and so forth. Rather then saying there's only one or two factors which are the catalyst for making a job change and leaving your present employment, let's simply agree there are several good reasons and it's up to each individual to decide what his/her decision is based upon. You must be the one to select the criteria for change.

Consider the following reasons for making a career change and see which one may or may not apply to you. Keep an open mind and be honest with yourself.

Reason One: There's a good chance your interests, likes, dislikes, attitudes, values, and feelings about your present job have changed considerably. You may also realize there is no turning around and covering ground you've already been over. You're dealing with a dead-ended street . . . you're up "cul de sac alley" with a bag over your head. The Faringi have landed! "Go to warp four, Mr. Crusher."

Reason Two: You've made a conscious decision to reevaluate your whole life. This decision has included a personal assessment of your needs, desires and any potential future

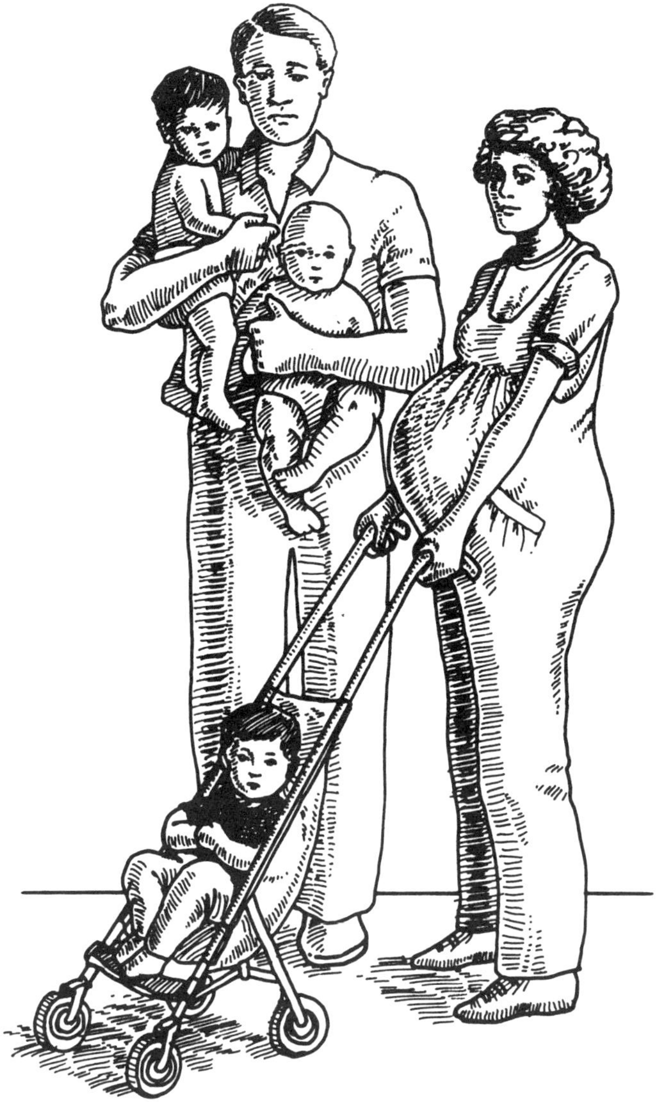

NOTES

career priorities. This is the time to refocus your present state of affairs and turn your attention directly to your career. You must begin to see the validity in making a change for your own betterment; and that may only be for peace of mind's sake.

Reason Three: Some unfortunate events have recently occurred in your life and the tragedies or traumas involved dictate a career change. However, you've already considered some alternatives and options, but the apparent need for a substantial change of jobs is imperative. Only you know those private reasons "why."

Reason Four: Your family is about to expand, or already has. In order to meet the anticipated increase of financial demands, a new career is in order. The focus now is on money; however, this could also be the time to consider other wants besides job security. For instance, more free time, freedom of responsibility, the flexibility to move about more, or a new exciting challenge.

Reason Five: Several things aren't going well at work and you've been passed over again for that long expected promotion or raise. Possibly you're about to be laid off or get fired. The company is closing down and/or moving to another state. One way or the other the events which are about to occur aren't in your favor and you don't see any light at the end of the tunnel which could be a reprieve or a saving grace.

Reason Six: You've aged! Maybe gracefully, maybe not. But you've recognized you aren't the same person you were last year and you want to redo yourself. You feel time is getting by you too quickly and there are some other things you'd like to try before it's too late. You know if you wait too long to make the changes you desire, well, they just won't happen. Therefore, you must act now with what you've already got, or at least intelligently prepare to make those essential life changes. Either way, you need to maintain control and do what your heart dictates. Remember to plan, plan, plan, so you won't fail in this undertaking. *If you fail to plan, you plan to fail!*

Reason Seven: You've come into a great deal of wealth, riches or resources which will allow you to excitedly explore new territory. Changing careers and/or becoming an entrepreneur looks appealing. Your new financial freedom can open some previously closed doors. If you plan on venturing forth and going through some of those open doors, be sure you map out your trip and effectively chart a course that will take you where you want to go. Just don't get lost along the way because of poor planning.

Reason Eight: You've already made your mark in your present career, and your accomplishments and achievements are numerous. You want to excel in some other field and you feel the urge to begin as soon as possible. However, you'll be leaving behind a successful track record and perhaps, a stunning stellar career. You reached heights where others envied your success, but the praise and prestige of your position and work are no longer the issue with you. They're secondary or may even be "history." You're not bothered by any unfinished business, you've closed the book on that chapter of your life and you've completed everything you wanted to finish. Now you choose to look into other exciting and perhaps, unrelated possibilities you've wanted to investigate for years. Go for it!

Reason Nine: You've "maxed out" in your career and there's literally no place else to go: upwards or laterally. You cannot expand, nor can you move into new areas of work, your job description prohibits such a possibility. You've reached the pinnacle of your job and there aren't any new challenges or opportunities left for you to pursue. Your ability for creativity and innovation is stifled; only the same old boring routine is slated for the future and you can't see wasting away many more years doing the same obnoxious tasks. It's unquestionably time to move on. If you don't make a change, you'll die a little each day as you continue performing the job you've learned to dislike.

Reason Ten: Your family is decreasing and your children are leaving home to get married, travel abroad, join the military, or get a job. They want to become independent. Perhaps, they've just completed college and your financial responsibilities are quickly diminishing. You can now find time and money to explore other career possibilities where you'll have less pressure, stress, and duties. However, you may also realize less money. But chances are you'll gain more freedom and have time to plan for a career which greatly interests you.

These aren't the only reasons for making significant changes in your life, but they are a start. Such reasons are some of the most noted situations, conditions or behaviors which have normally reflected attitudes that suggest the time is right to chance a career change. As you read through the options, you may have focused on one reason in particular which singled you out for a job change. Consider making the transition to something more exciting and perhaps, profitable. If there are two or three reasons which applied to you, try to work with them and plan for an effective career change. Don't sit on your duff and do nothing, be spirited and take some personal action.

> **Put your life's plan into determined action and go after what you want with all that's in you.**
> *Henry J. Kaise*

> **Hard work, discipline and focused effort usually result in a great accomplishment, a tremendous achievement or a most desirable profit.**
> *Jan Knox*

> **He who every morning plans the transactions of the day and follows out that plan, carries a thread that will guide him through the labyrinth of the most busy life. The orderly arrangement of his time is like a ray of light which darts itself through all his occupations. But where no plan is laid, where the disposal of time is surrendered merely to the chance of incidents, chaos will soon reign.**
> *Victor Hugo*

Changing professions should be fun. But you must plan effectively or you'll end up in a bucket of worms. When you decide to make a change, seek professional counseling, do it right, don't shoot pot luck from the hip and hope for the best. Vocational guidance counseling and training exist for your success. Counseling will aid you in making a very smooth transition from one career to your next.

Your Honest Evaluation

Most people don't want to take ownership for their present situation. They don't want to admit they're responsible for doing or not doing what they are or aren't doing in life. Who told you to be a grocery clerk, or a human resources director, or a car finisher, or a proctologist, or a sheet metal cutter?

Did your parents tell you to enter one of those professions? Did they say, "Hey kid of mine, you look like a sheet metal worker, so I think you better pursue that profession." Or were some simpler, more subtle suggestions given to you rather vicariously like (mother speaking to father), "Gee Harry, wouldn't it be nice if little Vickie became a proctologist when she gets older? You know, with all your trouble and medical problems."

Not too subtle, we know that . . . but do you? What got you to where you are today? What motivated and prompted you to become a barber, or a railroad engineer? Did you have assistance in determining how you would be working on an assembly line for "X" amount of years, or did you do that all by yourself? The only way you'll make progress in changing from one career to another is by "fessing up" as to "why" you are "where" you are today.

If the process was a good one, then you need to recognize that fact and move on from there. Of course, you can always use the same methods which worked for you the first time around. However, if you haven't a clue as to how you got where you are, or you say something profound like, "It just happened that way," then you're in big trouble and need some professional vocational guidance counseling.

Most people will use a medical specialist when they have some particular problem which requires the immediate attention of a specialist; or a consult a dentist for filling a broken tooth, or a carpenter to repair their patio covering, or a bookkeeper to handle their accounting needs, or a florist to do the flower arrangements for their daughter's wedding. But will they go to a vocational specialist (guidance counselor) to get professional assistance with their career needs? No, not usually. They'll go to Aunt Betty or Neighbor Raphael, or their good friend Sarah. Why? Because they are the respected resident experts. Didn't you know that? Yes, Betty and Raphael and Sarah have the answers for everything. So why shouldn't they be sought out for their expertise in career change?

This could well be the most important decision in your life, in fact it is your life, in a manner of speaking. Here's the sixty four dollar question, that's what folks used to say. Now it's simply, "What's happen,' wow, that's cool man. Ya gonna be ah usher where man? Yeh, that's totally rad vato," You get the picture, that's what's happening among most of our younger generation, who aren't getting proper counseling. Instead they seek the advice and approval of their illiterate and unschooled friends. Most folks simply don't seek proper counseling.

The key phrase herein is, "proper counseling," because you have the ability to recognize the need for it. Kids don't have that perspective or insight; they mostly flow with the tide, the gang, their friends, their feelings, and not with what is available and useful for them. So why should you settle for less too? Why should you have to put up with answers that come from friends and relatives? What do they know? Ask yourself that question very slowly, are they trained and educated in rendering to you exclusive professional career guidance? Probably not!

So, back to the vocational guidance counselor. Get one before you begin your journey to change your life. That's what career counselors are for, giving you direction based on knowledge and experience. Making this career change is extremely important to you. If it isn't, it should be or you shouldn't be considering making a change. Why? Because you're not serious enough; you're simply not into yourself and your future enough to care about what will happen to you. Think this decision out.

Come on Bubba, get real here! What are you talking about? This is your life, your potential professional career. Don't be kidding yourself about what you're probably going to do. You need to be honest with yourself and evaluate your present position. Then look at your options, if you know what they are. If you don't, then its time for professional advice. Prepare to go after it. If you don't, you probably won't make any significant effort toward changing your life and your career.

The averages and percentages of life show how your chances will be greatly diminished if you try to go it alone, or use Cousin Katherine's "for sure success formula." Don't procrastinate and don't seek out second or third rate advice. Go straight to the top and pay the price for hiring professionalism. Be prepared to make the right choices. And do it yesterday, not tomorrow.

> **Vacillating people seldom succeed. They seldom win the solid respect of their fellow men. Successful men and women are very careful in reaching decisions and very persistent and determined in action thereafter.**
> *L. G. Elliott*

Many career counselors claim there are three ways to get in synch with your destiny and you can find the right career path through using one of those methods. They are:

(1) Reviewing your childhood dreams and aspirations, ideals and visions of greatness or future achievement.

(2) Looking back over your education and the processes and content which delivered or suggested interesting things that promised satisfaction while meshing with your unrealized values; that is, a self-analysis of what truly turned you on during your formative school years.

(3) The alternative to numbers one and two is using professional guidance counseling and assistance: being tested and advised.

If we look at each of the above points, which do have merit and value, then you may learn something else about yourself. Something that can help you in determining what kind of a career move you really want to make. You may also uncover why you want to do what you eventually decide to do. Let's explore each potential pathway to your ideal career.

> It will take courage to cut away from the thousand and one hindrances that make life complex, but it can be done!
> *Rhoda Lacha*

> **Thousands of engineers can design bridges, calculate strains and stresses, and draw up specifications for machines, but the great engineer or administrator is the man who can tell whether the bridge or the machine should be built at all, where it should be constructed and when.**
> *E. G. Grace*

Pathway One: Do you recall the times when you were just becoming aware of the world around you and all the elements which made up its environment? Yes, you were part of a world that was changing and effecting your own young and unmolded psyche. All the information and attached circumstances involving that information went into your brain and was processed. You were becoming part and parcel of your own experiences. Some of those experiences were very good, others were not so pleasant.

You need to recover the memory of those good experiences and the unique information attached to that memory. For example, if you had a bad experience with a trash collector, or a garbage man, and your collective memory recalls only the bad behaviors or experiences associated with that "flashback," then there's a terrific chance you won't become a sanitary engineer. Oh, the wonderful power of euphemisms.

If you were bitten by a dog, and a cat, or some other animal, there's a good chance you won't be very partial to the field of veterinary medicine. It's highly doubtful you'll be behind the counter of a pet store or studying animal husbandry. This doesn't mean you hate being around animals, besides, you may have several pets; however, you won't be among the crowd applying for admittance into the university's Zoology program, nor will you be found standing in line waiting to be hired for a Game Warden's job. And when your youngest child wants her first puppy, you'll be wishing you could buy a "daget" from the gift store onboard the Battlestar Galactica.

When you were in the second grade, your teacher stopped at your desk and told you how ugly your painting was. She said it looked like a dead frog. You never forgot that incident; especially because the picture was your impression of a beautiful prancing horse. Your feelings were crushed. Your chances of becoming a free impressionist painter are rather bleak, so are your chances of doing many creative things that might include using a paint brush or similar tools.

Yet, on the positive side, you were told by your seventh grade teacher how good your creative story was, captivating his attention and making him feel part of the action. Thus, journalism or literature may be your bag, or perhaps something in communications and the speech arts may grab your attention. Your experience was a positive experience. It made you aware of how much potential you had in doing something that initially may not have been your cup of tea. But now, after looking backwards, you've got to admit, there's room for consideration and further exploration.

When your knowledge and experiences have proven to be positive and enlightening, and you find yourself engaged in checking out a career closely aligned with such past experiences, there's an excellent chance you'll find something satisfying about becoming part of a career which deals directly or indirectly with those "good feeling" emotions and thoughts.

Digging up the dreams. We always tell our clients to go back to the rudimentary stages of their lives and conjure up those old feelings which meant so much, but for some reason were left neglected and discarded. Your dreams of the past were some of your first endeavors to connect your real life experiences with the creative genius inside your brain. The better you connected those two separate elements, the more extraordinary your thoughts and talents probably became.

> **There is one thing over which each person has absolute, inherent control, and that is his mental attitude.**
> *W. Clement Stone*

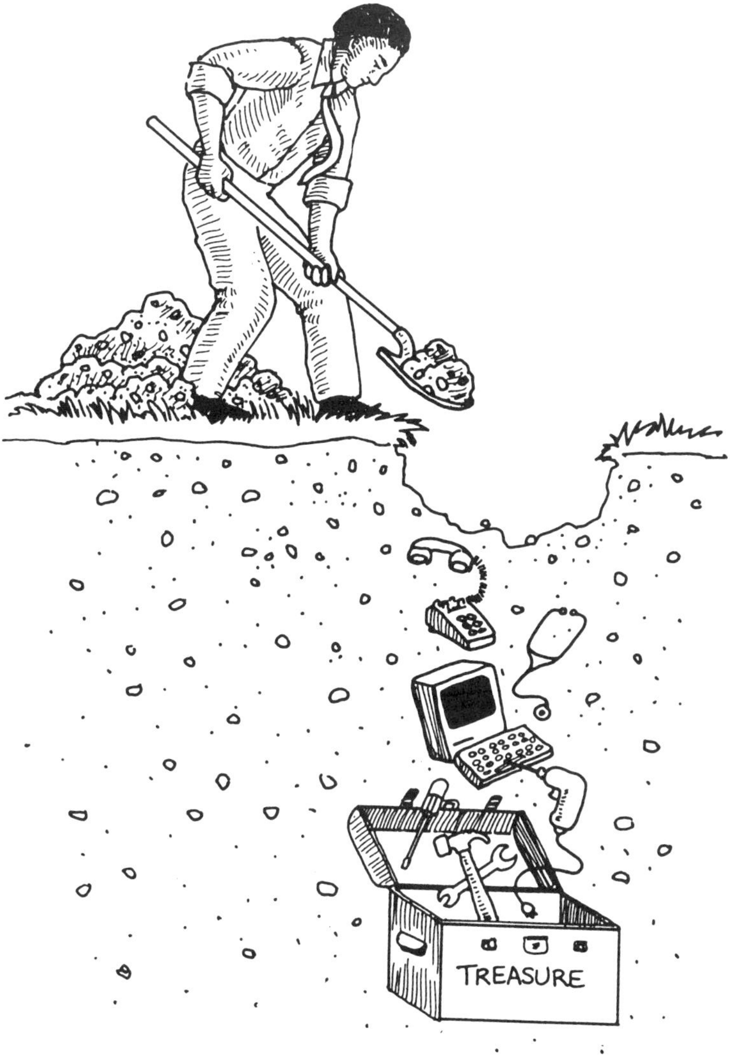
TREASURE

NOTES

During World War II, the country was preoccupied with the events of the war and what the outcome would be. There never seemed to be much doubt about how things would turn out. Folks always spoke about this general and that general and this victory and that victory, and how our marines would be triumphant in the Pacific Theater, and so forth.

When you're just a toddler and hear such things and see magazine pictures about some distant battle called a "war," you imagine all sorts of sordid glorious, yet devilish happenings. Many of those mental images can be very scary and upsetting yet other images can promote mental pictures of glory and power. Well, what do toddlers know about such things? Let me tell you Bucko, kids aren't stupid, but they are very impressionable.

Dahk's Personal Experience: I wasn't a real smart child, but neither was I any mother's dummy. I was just average in intelligence and I matured like the normal boy my age. In other words, there wasn't anything special about me, Good Lord, my mother would faint if she ever read this book! However, I needed to set the stage for the mediocrity of my puerile being.

What was interesting about this whole story was how the comments of war effected my thinking and helped create and develop images in my mind that were cluttered thoughts ensconced with visions of soldiering and sailoring. As I listened to the adults speak about distant battles, famous military officers, tanks and B-29s, my head filled with graphic scenes which included a cloudy vision of my adult self, at the helm of my own tank leading a weary company of tired and tattered infantry men into combat.

Guess what happened next? I know, you really don't care about baby Dahk's dreams, but this is what you need to understand to see how the process works. And it will work for you, if once you understand it, you let it. Baby Dahk found a big empty cardboard box and climbed into it. It became his tank, his armored car, his airplane, his miniature battleship and whatever he needed it to be at the moment of his "imaging enactments."

What are "imaging enactments?" They're horrible little animals that feed on unsuspecting children. Just kidding. They're fanciful dreams being played out as though real. Like when you had an imaginary playmate and together you sailed the oceans and conquered exotic lands and slew evil giants. Well, my Puff was a magic cardboard box and I was utterly invincible. But, the final coup de grace was when I recognized and saw myself as General Knox. If you asked me what I was going to be when I grew up, your answer would've been an immediate, "Brigadier General." Little wonder I answer to the title of Commander when I'm involved in Naval Reserve activities. Before that, it was Lieutenant and Staff Sergeant and Airman Basic and Mr. Nobody. Well, we all have our roots, don't we?

The point of the story was to show you, through personal experience how I was "unconsciously molded in my childhood beliefs and fantasies." By taking in information during my formative years and applying it to my psyche, it eventually dictated certain parameters for my future behaviors and career goals. Although I never proactively pursued becoming a brigadier general, I did become more than involved in spending a great deal of my life, over thirty years, directly or vicariously wrapped up in military activities. So much for Dahk.

Personal Experience Example Two: We're still working within the parameters of Pathway One, so let's take a closer look at another person's life using our first method.

We find the experiences of our next subject very interesting. We'll call her Suzy. Suzy grew up in a Japanese-American family of medical doctors and dentists. They lived in Santa Barbara, California. During World War II, Suzy's family had been subjected to the debasing internment procedures levied, by the United States government, upon her and her family.

During her internment, Suzy learned to live with less than she had previously become accustomed to having. Although her young life had changed dramatically over night, Suzy still managed to adapt to her new surroundings and environment. As most children assimilate well into any society, Suzy made her transformation with very little concern or worry.

Conversations among the adults usually turned to the course of the Pacific War and their own miserable situations of "lock up." Suzy heard stories of discrimination, although it wasn't something spoken of very much in the early 1940s. She heard utterings of degradation and poor treatment by Anglo-Americans, and she heard whispers about distant relatives who were suffering in Japan. Suzy didn't know those relatives, she'd never been to Sapporo, Misawa or Chitose. They were only foreign places to her and so were her Japanese cousins and "sui generis."

As time passed, Suzy began to take to heart the delicate feelings of her family and their closest Japanese-American friends. One theme seemed to permeate every story; it was of shame and guilt, but it was surrounded by fear, misunderstanding and distrust. Suzy was only about seven years old when she left the camp with her family. But those unwelcomed memories of the three plus years she'd experienced of being a second class, distrusted citizen had left their mark.

Suzy had watched her parents, both medical doctors, be forced to accept inner camp work as glorified Red Cross aids, hardly ever getting to practice their trade in the manner they'd known before. There wasn't a great deal of work for her father the Internist, nor for her mother the Neurologist. And her oldest brother Brad, the dentist with only one year of practice under his belt, never had an opportunity to fill one tooth. He was assigned to a menial job handling clerical matters for the camp's Military Police unit.

So what thoughts went through Suzy's mind? Why all the background on Suzy's family? The background is important because it set the stage for educating Suzy about how unfair life can be and how most people didn't care about her race, because they were Oriental, specifically Japanese. Unfortunately, every Japanese in America became a subject of ridicule and distrust. Suzy had witnessed most of those awful behaviors and had desperately tried to make sense out of what was occurring around her.

That's extremely difficult for such a young child and especially one who'd hardly had a chance to know the wonderful normalcy of being part of a family with supposedly unalienable liberties. A family who lived in their own house and ran their own lives the way they'd seen fit. Suzy became quickly acquainted with a world that was filled with hardship and pain, distress and worry, fearing the unknown and having to do without even some of the simplest luxuries life afforded to others.

Suzy eventually left the internment camp with her family. They moved to a new part of the state, settling in Oceanside, California. Her family gradually reclaimed its dignity. The material wealth they once had slowly made its way back into her life again. You'd think with all the possible medical or dental talk occurring around the house, that perhaps Suzy would've possibly been influenced into becoming a doctor of sorts.

That wasn't the hand life dealt Suzy, it wasn't even close. After several years of going to college, Suzy received her degree in Business, with a strong emphasis in Accounting. After graduation, Suzy joined her brother's dental practice as an office manager and bookkeeper. On the side, she built up a small accounting clientele and began to study income tax preparation.

Six years later, Suzy went out on her own and opened her own Tax and Bookkeeping Service. For 27 years she did very well, but when she turned 55 she became extremely depressed about her life and what she'd done with it. She had tremendous difficulty justifying how she'd spent so many years (33), involved in the tax and accounting business. She regretted not doing something which was more meaningful to her. At least something she said that was, "more exciting and dealt with helping people."

The year was 1990 and Suzy had just turned 55 years old two weeks before she came to see us. We discussed numerous aspects of her personal and professional life and listened very diligently as Suzy poured forth a plethora of information. Suzy was desperate for a career change. Not only did her emotional behavior reflect such a needed change but her testing results, measured on the Occupational Stress Inventory, were "maxed out" and also indicated the need for a major vocational career move.

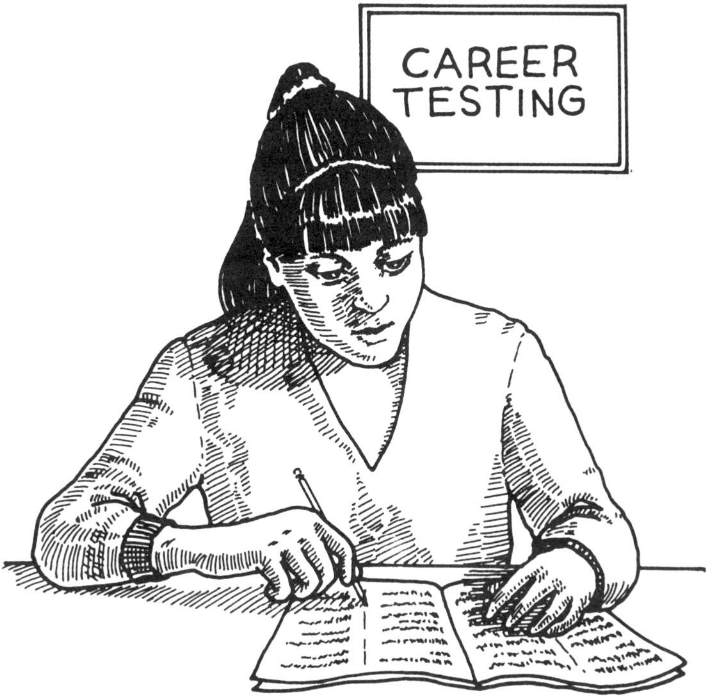
CAREER
TESTING

NOTES

One of the first procedures we do with new clients after our up-front introductions, counseling program description, and an initial assessment and evaluation, is to administer various batteries of vocational tests. The tests selected are determined by our professional opinions concerning the client and what examination tool will best serve the client's needs.

Part of that process is reserved for taking the Occupational Stress Inventory. We feel if the client's scores are relatively high, falling above the "high stress" level and well into the "maladaptive stress" level, in both the organizational stress and psychological strain categories, and if the client's coping resource scores fall into the "mild deficit" or "significant lack" categories, then we usually preclude doing any vocational guidance counseling or career development until after the client gets his or her life into better order. That may mean making some significant life style or career changes on their own, like extended vacation time, a leave of absence or undergoing professional clinical therapy.

Once testing has been completed and a case file has been opened, we begin career mapping or pathing. Part of that process is going backwards and looking at many various aspects of a person's life. This encompasses speaking about the various past geographical locations where one has lived. It also looks at the individual's educational, working and social environments which were experienced during the same time frames.

By exploring where one has lived, studied and interacted, it becomes possible to segment one's attitudinal beliefs and feelings into two groups: positive and negative. The idea is to find what turns a person on and what turns a person off. The focus of this phase of the counseling is to define and isolate areas of a person's learning experiences, social activities and environmental settings which were pleasurable and encouraging for the client.

When negativisms pop out in the open, we also isolate them into another special group, one that we hope to avoid when trying to piece together a new career pathway. Every client wants the ideal vocation to jump up and materialize in front of them; unfortunately, it doesn't happen that way. It takes time, work and effort, and a combined team effort (of client and counselor) working together towards building a new future career. Part of that process is also eliminating bad or non-productive and non-agreeable experiences. In other words, we get rid of the fat and gristle and go for the tender cut; how it's prepared is part of the personal choice portion of the vocational pathing process.

Success is 99% mental attitude. It calls for love, joy, optimism, confidence, serenity, poise, faith, courage, cheerfulness, imagination, initiative, tolerance, honesty, humility, patience and enthusiasm.
Wilfred Peterson

So, noting Suzy's feelings about her past and where she lived, studied and socialized was quite rewarding. It was rich in data and served us all with a great deal of information to sift through and find values, interests and potential career directions. We did this very effectively in Suzy's case and learned something about her forgotten dreams.

Suzy had been deeply touched by the misery and unhappiness which had surrounded her during her family's internment, and for several difficult years afterwards. It's quite hard for many people to forgive and forget, and although the war had ended years before, there was still lingering feelings of animosity and prejudice affecting Suzy's world. Not unlike the vicarious Japan-bashing spillover indirectly suffered by Kristi Yamaguchi, which may have lessened her gold medal chances of participating in product endorsements, but similar. Unspoken words and less than positive behaviors add up to feelings which interpret non-verbal actions as a lack of support. They are negativisms.

The idea of helping others overcome their grief, misery, pains, anxiety and misfortunes had greatly interested Suzy but she never pursued a profession which kept her in constant contact with people who needed her assistance. Instead, Suzy did just the opposite and chose a career field which would keep her relatively isolated from the pain of society. She got lost in numbers because is was safe territory and human contact was always at a minimum. Numbers shielded Suzy for over 33 years. It was time to step out from behind the facade she had erected and become the person she had once thought she could become.

We hadn't solved anything as yet, we still had a long way to go in order to fully examine all the data we had collected and to further collect more information about other elements of Suzy's background and current life.

Viewing and discussing a person's developed skills and competencies is a section of the vocational career pathing process which needs careful consideration. Most clients believe they have either acquired skills or competencies from learning environments or situational training. However, the acquisition of skills, competencies and knowledge is an accumulation of many contributing factors. Suzy learned she'd developed some of her skills and competencies from watching her mother, or other revered people who did things she admired and from whom she'd desired to learn. She also became aware of how she'd developed special skills from focused training sessions and skill specific workshops. She eventually realized everything she could do well had a learning origin.

Although we couldn't identify all of Suzy's learning origins, we did make successful progress in turning up several sources of her inspiration and instruction. Of course these came from close friends, relatives, neighbors, teachers and others who had taken the time to show Suzy how to do certain tasks and so forth. The motivation to do those tasks was usually centered in Suzy's own personal desire to learn and achieve without boundaries, free from inhibitions and negative influences. Education in the classroom had been a large part of Suzy's skill and knowledge foundation.

In a client's quest for a new career, we usually have to go back to their beginnings and start with the basics. We know you didn't want to hear that, but it's true. That's where you root out the original interests, appeals, stimulants and influences which are usually long forgotten.

> **Quiet minds cannot be perplexed or frightened, but go on in fortune and misfortune at their own private pace, like a clock during a thunderstorm.**
> *Robert Lewis Stevenson*

Suzy's appeals and interests were still making her look more like someone who would've entered a healing art or science profession, like her parents. But medicine wasn't for Suzy, so she started considering many of the various fringe professions. The two vocations which attracted her attention the most were, counseling and social work.

Suzy didn't settle immediately on either profession, she was only part of the way through her vocational career pathing. She hadn't yet taken the time to explore her emotional side. We asked her to spend time thinking about her particular feelings as they concerned specific subjects. If she objected to being around people who had lots of personal problems, and if she thought she'd feel the strain and exhaustion caused by other's needs, which could take a heavy toll on her personal life as well as her professional life, then careers calling for much self-sacrifice and involvement wouldn't be for her.

We also made Suzy aware of how her personal beliefs could get in the way of her professional duties if they crossed over lines of personal ethics or values. Our examples were of a religious nature. That's where most of our clients have had problems with their careers. Careers come into conflict with spiritual beliefs. Some religions have convictions which don't allow them to sway from their seeded beliefs; therefore, those beliefs may interfere with the proper and expected performance of a client's job. It's a strong consideration which oftentimes changes a person's mind about pursuing a particular career. It just depends on how important the career is compared to the theocratical belief of the client.

There are numerous examples, so to cite just a few consider the following:

(1) A Jewish ball player may not participate in a game on a specified holy day he or she must observe.

(2) A Seventh-Day Adventist will not sell his or her products on Saturday, one of the biggest sales days of the week, because of religious observances.

(3) A Jehovah's Witness will not accept a government job because of theological beliefs.

The list goes on and on.

How about ethics and values? There isn't much sense in compromising these personal attributes either. Leastwise, not if you're serious about sticking to your guns and holding true to your beliefs. Why should you sell a product that you don't believe in? How well do you think you would do? Your sales would most likely be very low. Or could you work with people you feel are dishonest and lack integrity? Could you be made to behave in such a way that your job or profession became very unnatural or uncomfortable for you?

If you want to be successful, don't ever compromise your personal or professional ethics or values. Maintain high standards and traditions which make you feel good about yourself and your life. Don't ever step out of vogue for the sake of doing something which will lower you in your own eyes.

After Suzy reviewed her spiritual and emotional side, she began to focus on special types of things she enjoyed doing, besides those items we'd previously covered during her skill and competency portion of the counseling. We also took a close look at the types of people Suzy liked to be around.

Initially we tried to segregate certain activities that pleased Suzy the most. Then we prioritized those activities and quantified their personal worth to Suzy, indicating how important they were to her over other activities. After that, we did the exact same thing with the types of people Suzy wanted to be around. What was exceptionally interesting, was that the type of person Suzy liked to be associated with was quite different from the ilk of individual with whom Suzy eventually chose to work.

On one hand, Suzy liked to be with other Asian-American friends and relatives, mostly interacting and socializing. Her ideal situation was to be engaged in reflective conversation which put her in the mainstream of the subject and acknowledged her as an expert consultant. Her thirty plus years of consultation had definitely left its mark...and that's okay, as long as it remains or becomes a plus and not a negative or a minus in a new career formula. It wasn't seen as a negative for Suzy. In fact, it was a tremendous plus.

Suzy chose to get her act together in a systematic, organized manner. She decided she wanted to become a social worker. The people she'd be dealing with wouldn't be near the type of individual she wanted to spend her free time with. In fact, she saw those extreme differences as a sort of balancing factor in her life. We felt if that's what she wants, and if that's what she believes and makes her happy, then it'll probably work out well for Suzy. It's simple, if it works for Suzy, it works for us! This isn't a form of unsophistocated vocational magic, it's all choice and personal selection.

After Suzy decided to prepare for a career change which lead to eventual licensing in clinical social work, we started Suzy working with her **Personal Profile Plan**. This plan provides a clear pathway for future success when making a career change. We use this with all of our clients and college students. We also use the **Personal Profile Plan** for training purposes and projecting significant future changes in other dimensions of personal and professional life. The plan was especially designed to assist individuals in making major life changes or transitions.

In summary, Suzy selected a profession she wants, while being able to use her best and most significant talents. Suzy wants to finish her schooling and internship then work for a few years with a state agency or private hospital, and afterwards go into private practice. She isn't considering retiring in her sixties.

Good, competent social workers, who have established a track record and a name for themselves, can pull down over $60,000 a year. Mediocrity will only net you 30K or so. Suzy wasn't as concerned about the money she could make as she was about career satisfaction. Being happy at what she did was Suzy's bottomline.

> *The Law of Happiness:* **A life of earthly success is full of perils and anxieties. If a man does not have the elements of happiness within himself, not all of the beauty and variety, the pleasures and interests of the whole world can give it to him.**
> *Alfred Armand Montapert*

Pathway Two: A self-analysis of what truly turned you on during your formative school years, can usually evoke old feelings and desires which have been buried for years. Similar to what Suzy did, this second choice places the bulk of its focus on digging up or resurrecting long expired bones. Bones, in the sense of being treasured dreams, which in another sense have been buried and forgotten. We're going to ask you to go back into your past and try to remember places, things and people you liked being around and/or being a part of so long ago.

One good example, would be trying to recall a special Summer you spent at camp, or living with a relative in a different state or country. Perhaps it was during Fall or Winter when you went to live with Aunt Jane because your father and mother went to Europe on business, or your mother may have died when you were young, so Aunt Jane asked your father for permission for you to spend an extra long vacation with her. The possibilities are almost endless and we've all had plenty of them. Try to dig those dreams and experiences out of your mind. This takes a committed effort from you, don't just sit there and after 20 seconds say, "I give up, I can't think of anything useful." That's a cop-out, concentrate and focus on a specific time in your past. This isn't difficult.

It never ceases to amaze us how many people, who when they first come to us, claim they haven't had any past experiences from which they can draw. They try to puzzle something positive together out of nothing. The fact of the matter is that they haven't really tried to think back. They expect old memories and thoughts to instantly pop into their heads and lay out answers and information in front of their noses. It just doesn't happen that way. Please don't try to kid yourself into thinking otherwise. If you do, you'll be one lost puppy.

The idea here is to focus your thoughts back to a special time in your life. A time representative of the only happy moments you had as a child, or young adult. There are people who's lives have been filled with tragedy or grief and believe us, they have some tough digging to do. Occasionally, we have to use **Pathway Three** for them: being tested and advised. Why? Because they simply can't focus back far enough to dig up the material we need to use, or they just haven't had the kind of experiences necessary for vocational career pathing.

Some folks have come out of broken homes. Their childhood and formative school years were periods of misery and anger. They were either abused, unloved, or thrown out to the wolves. Many times we've listened to some terrible case scenarios. So **Pathway Three** is the vehicle to use when all else fails to produce tangible and substantial data for development, analysis and exploration. Whatever you do, don't try to force the issue and make something out of something that just isn't there, be sensible.

So let's go back to talking about places, things and people. They're the three identified topics which have seemed to produce more rich information for background study and consideration than have any other experiential elements of one's past.

One such case example is Richard. He lived a rather disjointed childhood which came to a rapid end at thirteen. He was a product of a broken marrage with a wayward mother who had little education and knowledge of how to survive in

West Texas. In search of a better life and an easier living, Richard's mother moved the family to central California and Richard got his first taste of becoming relatively self-supporting. He had to work in order to assist his mother and supplement their income.

In a short period of time, Richard's mother met a man and moved back to Texas. Richard ended up staying in California, he liked working on the farm; it was his first taste of real security. There wasn't any place for him in his mother's new life and Richard knew it. In time, he missed his mother and moved back to West Texas. He found out how difficult it was to make a living in the dust bowl. He floated from one job to another. He was barely able to keep his head above water in school. Although he'd never quit going to class, his trek through life as a part time worker and full time student had taken its toll.

Richard considered his alternatives. He lied about his age and joined the Navy. Once in the Navy he was able to get "three squares" and a warm bunk. He was able to strike for a rating which interested him and in time he learned to love his new found home and source of employment. He even took a liking to his job. Richard had finally found a purpose. Prior to the Navy, he'd lost any hope of having a better life. The military was his turn around, it educated and trained him.

Now we could go on from here and talk more about Richard and you'd eventually learn how he became a successful Electronics Engineer who had a great future. He'd been blessed with a nice family, especially his loving and devoted wife. Then you'd learn about his eventual collapse and attempt at recovery. That's the point where we came into Richard's life. But the lesson here is about finding out what could be extracted from Richard's past to be used in opening up a new world of potential achievement for Richard. He needed a new horizon very badly; something to cling to and make work for himself. So we dug. Now that took time and considerable effort.

The initial hours spent with Richard were used to dig up and resurrect past items of interest. We had Richard tell us about everything he did or was involved with from the time things started to mean something to him. That is, from the time Richard began to take an interest in performing various actions, or participating in this activity and that activity. The result was encouraging.

At one time in Richard's childhood, an uncle rebuilt car parts: generators, pumps and so forth. He also worked on electrical car systems. Richard would watch his uncle take a customer's broken car part into his shop and disassemble it, then restore it to working order and feel great about making it work like new again.

Richard quickly learned how to do various small jobs by simply watching what his uncle did. On occasion, his uncle would let Richard soak and scrub some of the parts and make them look bright and shiny. In time, Richard even got to use some tools to perform a small number of the easier tasks repairing some of the less difficult parts. Eventually, Richard was allowed to disassemble this part or that and sometimes try to repair it without supervision.

When Richard finished each job, he'd take it to his uncle who would inspect his work and tell him how well he'd done. No matter what had to be reworked by his uncle, his uncle never said anything but good comments to Richard. On a reworked piece of equipment, his uncle would simply say something like, "Good job Ricky, but you know what, I think I'll just use a little of uncle's Ed's magic and make this just a tiny bit more copacetic." Richard never knew what copacetic meant, and he said he never asked. He just knew it meant something good, something very special. Then his uncle said, "We sure do some good work together, don't we Ricky?" Richard would agree and be satisfied. Besides, he'd done most of the good work and uncle Ed was just going to put the final finishing touches on it.

Uncle Ed died of a heart attack when Richard was only nine years old. He loved Ed, but with his uncle's passing, so went Uncle Ed's repair shop business. A few months later, Richard and his mother were on their way to Odessa, Texas. His mother had a job in a roadside cafe and Richard became bored again. A neighbor who had a garage not far from the cafe wouldn't even allow Richard to hang around and watch him or his hired help work.

In time, Richard moved on to other interests, but none as meaningful as putting things back together and making them

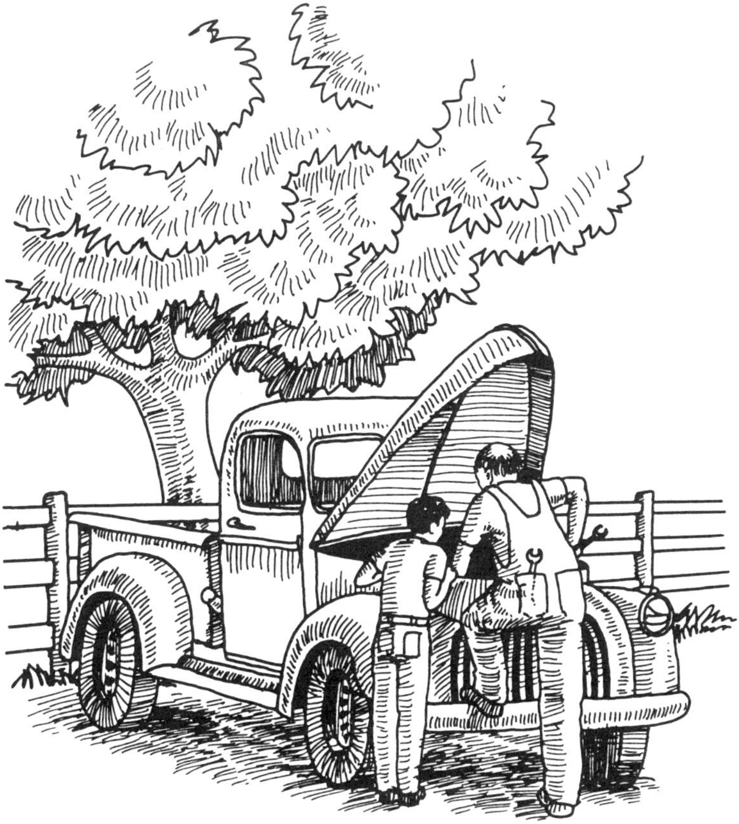

NOTES

work again. The closest he'd come to fixing things would be when he entered the Navy and officially learned a new trade.

Thirty seven years had passed since Richard first worked on a piece of car equipment. Many new items had replaced the old car parts Richard remembered; however, the interest of making something new or fixing something old was still in his blood. This love wouldn't be taken from him. You've heard of the expression, "You can take me out of Texas, but you can't take Texas out of me." Well, you could take the opportunity of repairing things away from Richard, but he'd never lose his love for fiddling with the broken parts.

Richard was determined to begin a second career. He was in his mid-forties and just coming off a year of medical leave. He'd had a long time to recuperate from his illness and that time period allowed him ample opportunity to think about doing something he wanted to do. Going back into electronics was not for Richard. However, doing something he wanted to do while being able to use his electronic skills and abilities was ideal for Richard. He'd become excited about the new possibilities and his new sense of conviction for a change in careers.

The thought of becoming a small business owner intrigued Richard. He loved the sea and boats; nautical equipment had always held a special place in his heart. So putting four and four together could mean a real success story if he devised a plan and if the plan worked out. He decided to become an electronics repairman for nautical equipment.

Richard's first step was to concoct a business plan. Part of that plan was going to see potential clientele, boat owners who may need his services. Not knowing who those owners might be, Richard decided to survey the various boat marinas in the local area. He started in San Diego and worked his way up to Newport-Balboa. Along the way, he interviewed two other gentlemen who were listed in the Yellow Pages for doing electronics repair on nautical equipment. Both individuals tried to discourage Richard by telling him how tough it was to get business and stay in business. But somehow their stories didn't seem to wash.

Apparently the business was good, good enough to allow both men to have their own repair shops and stores. A third party would mean less of a market share of repair business for them. It would equate to more proactive sales effort and solicitation and provide a bigger challenge for both men. Obviously they were comfortable where they were; they didn't want any new competition but times change.

Richard decided to go for it. If two men could do so well and have all the business along the Southern California coast, then why shouldn't Richard try for his corner of the repair market? Richard took up the challenge to go after the work.

The point of this example is that Richard used his already existing talents to do something he wanted to do on his own terms. He got to set his hours and decide on where and with who he wanted to work. He got to call the shots and this was possible because he had the skills and expertise to deliver the goods!

What Richard did was review his own abilities and assess certain activities he enjoyed doing. He like the sea and things associated with the sea and he made a conscious decision that he'd do something somehow connected to boats and water. He felt his skills with electronics went without question, so all he needed to find out was what the realistic possibilities were of him getting some substantial repair business.

Richard also knew he could custom build various devices which would or could be used on board sea-going vessels. His target market became private boat owners; folks who had boats with problem equipment. After spending many mornings and afternoons around the docks, moorings and marinas, Richard started getting his first business calls. Within a short period of time, his business started to increase and word spread concerning his expertise. His work was considered to be grade "A" quality and he finished his jobs either on time or ahead of time. People were satisfied and Richard became successful, and his pleasant demeanor didn't hurt business either. His good nature and cheerfulness paid-off.

Richard dug deeply to find all the pieces he needed for his career puzzle. The repair element came from deep in his past and linked up with his love for water and nautical things. From his naval electronic skills, to his current abilities and knowledge about engineering, his own tailored career was fashioned.

> Promotion awaits the employee who radiates
> cheerfulness, not the employee who spreads
> gloom and dissatisfaction. Doctors tell us that
> cheerfulness is an invaluable aid to health.
> Cheerfulness is also an invaluable
> aid to promotion.
> B. C. Forbes

> The health of the eye seems to depend
> on a horizon. We are never tired so
> long as we can see far enough.

Pathway Three: Tested and advised. Sometimes **Pathway One** and **Pathway Two** aren't the proper routes to go when counseling a client. For all the reasons, which were already covered in the first two pathways, the third pathway is almost unaffected by them and is somewhat different and less involved with a client's past. The bent of this pathway is to administer various testing tools, instruments or vehicles and measure the results. Upon measuring the results and assessing the findings, the next step is to inform the client of what you've determined. Testing occurs during the third, or third and fourth sessions with the client.

The first meeting is for discussing what the client is seeking, identifying the counseling methods to be used and laying out the payment terms. Meeting two is for data gathering, such as an initial intake and assessment; meetings three and four, as mentioned above, are for administering various testing batteries; meeting five could also be used for more test batteries (if necessary) or for discussing the results of the previous testing tools, and/or for setting down a counseling plan which should work for the client.

When session number five begins, **Pathway Three** really kicks in. With its purpose defined by the prior meetings, counseling takes the form of assisting the client in determining his or her future career. It accomplishes this while providing ongoing support, instruction and aid which helps the client progress toward that goal in an effective manner. This process takes time and must be handled with extreme diligence and concern. This is the vocational career pathing of someone's life. It's very serious and involved. If a counselor is involved only superficially in advising the client, then the counselor's approach is not adequate, nor will it be as effective as it should be.

The third pathway is structured so the client is able to discern various interest areas without having to dig into the past and pull up ideas. The counselor should provide the client with all available materials which engender enthusiasm and interest in the world around him. When clients cannot present themselves with confidence and lack a background rich in experience, it becomes the job of the counselor to furnish enough information and ideas, so that the client has alternatives and options from which to choose.

Those options shouldn't be so many that the client cannot decide and becomes further confused. The client must be able to make some respectable choices from within interest groupings that have captivated his or her interest and propelled them towards certain career areas. **Pathway Three** provides professional counseling materials as aids and assists the client in initially determining what is of interest, and secondly, how it can be fruitful in his or her life. The ideal would be to present as many aspects of a certain profession as is possible and then explore the good and the bad of each profession.

Although job satisfaction should be the bottomline, sometimes for a client to reach that point they are staring at one or more of *the four big "P's" first: position, prestige, power or profit.* It's considered okay to have the big "P's" as goals, but one should counsel the client on achieving some balance; that is, getting a shot of realistic equilibrium. A little of this and a little of that, rather than all of one goal and none of another.

For example: mix some profit with position and job satisfaction; or mix some power and prestige with job satisfaction, or mix some power and profit with job satisfaction, or mix some position and prestige with job satisfaction. Just don't let the final outcome be one of simple job satisfaction without a big "P." You must achieve some balance so the client will be well rounded. There is nothing worse than loving what you are doing and having to give it up because you aren't making any money. That is an example of pure job satisfaction with a balancing big "P." Most first time career changers need money to survive and pay bills, as do many second career changers or retired individuals trying something new. Most people need a mixture of the big "P's" with their portion of job satisfaction; so be ready to condone it.

Or, what about a job with lots of power and profit, but no decent business ethics or social morality factored into the success equation, and thus, no balance, no job satisfaction. The counseling principle is fairly easy. *The prime objective of the counselor is to assist the client in finding not only a suitable vocation, but one which is a career that provides a balance of job satisfaction with one or more of the big "P's."*

> Nature does not give to those who will not spend; her gifts are loaned to those who will use them. Empty your lungs and breathe. Run, climb, work and laugh, the more you give out the more you shall receive. Participate. Men do not really live for honors or for pay; their happiness is not in the taking and holding, but in the doing, the striving, the building, the serving.
> *Harry Marsh*

NOTES

LOOKING AHEAD TO THE FUTURE

The Cycle Of Vocational Growth:
Professional Growth Through Change

Life in general is composed of many different types of cycles. The first cycle we become aware of is time. We get up in the morning and we go to bed in the evening, and the next day the same cycle begins all over again. When we enter school we start in September and end in June, unless we are part of another educational program. If we are, or have been, then we were part of a six week cycle, or something similar.

Professional sports have yearly cycles. In baseball, Spring training starts in late February, goes to early April and then the season begins. It ends in October, after the World Series. Professional football is similar. It's season begins with its first league games in September and climaxes with the Super Bowl in late January. Most universities and colleges run their academic programs in cycles of quarters, semesters or monthly starts; it all depends on where you're enrolled.

The military likes to have its people transferred every two or three years, once again depending on which service you're stationed. Even the female body goes through a monthly cycle and men go from being little boys to men and back to little boys again. Our universe is composed of cycles: consider the planetary orbits around the sun and the passings of 75 year cycle comets. The list is truly endless. We grow up in a world of cycles, so why not allow ourselves to use the cycle system to our advanges? It's obvious that we understand its workings and feel relatively acquainted with and accustomed to its behaviors: beginning, middle and end. Let's make the cycle work for us in our personal and professional lives.

To do this, we have to ask ourselves a series of questions. These questions are part and parcel of the cycle itself. The particular cycle we're interested in is geared to our professional growth. *The questions should be examined with care and vision.* Without either of these two elements you'll not be successful in establishing a professional growth cycle that's the least bit valuable to yourself. The key words once again are: care and vision.

The questions are grouped into three divisions. These divisions are called states. The Present State, the Future State and the Transitional State. The Present State deals with all aspects of your life as it is now. The Future State defines where you want to be in "X" amount of time (usually years) and what you want to be doing. The Transitional State is the most difficult phase to go through; its posture is continuous and demanding, it holds you to your agreement with yourself and requires dedicated effort.

The Present State

(1) The Present State identifies your job and breaks it down into definable elements of importance by prioritizing your responsibilities and duties, in terms of percentages.

    a. Management practices; i.e., direct supervision - 70%
    b. Administrative tasks; i.e., reporting, paperwork - 13%
    c. Customer service; i.e., front desk, telephone - 9%
    d. Computer skills; i.e., data entry, dBase 3+ log - 6%
    e. External accounts; i.e., sales calls, follow-up - 2%

The Present State also reviews your personal life and requires you to assess the following areas and provide each phase with definition and clarity. You need to know where you are before you can start going someplace else. How else will you be able to know how to get where you desire to go?

(2) The first concern of your personal life to be discussed is your family relationship. Everybody in your family counts and has a say so. If you don't recognize this and give each one a chance to voice their own personal opinion, then you may never have consensus for your decision. Make your family part of this transition and they'll always be there to help you through the tough spots. This begins with explaining what you want to do with your life, right up front. Share your ideals and strive for a complete family buy-in. You'll need them on your side. Identify the correct answers to the following items:

a. Your family's feelings about a career change.
b. What obstacles they feel you'll encounter.
c. What they are willing to contribute towards your plan.
d. What is in it for them.
e. How they fit into your big picture.
f. What they see happening along the way.
g. How supportive they are of your transition.
h. Their positives and negatives.
i. What your transition will demand of them: their opinion.
j. What they see as the final outcome.
k. What their hidden agendas may be.
l. Write down and save their expectations.

(3) Take the time to evaluate the hours you spend away from the workplace; in particular, doing things for yourself. This could be time spent in an avocation, a second job, assisting in Little League or Girl Scouts, doing yard work (which may be a hobby) or other significant amounts of time that go into something other than your family or your job. That time must be identified and accounted for, all those hours have been valuable enough to you in the past, so they have relevance and worth. Besides, you'll need those hours in the future for more important tasks and responsibilities.

When you have completed items (1), (2) and (3), you'll be ready to answer the first group of questions, those belonging to the Present State.

(1) Who am I?
(2) Where am I?
(3) What am I doing here?
(4) How did I get where I am?
(5) What do I do next? (This answer should incorporate your plans for defining your expected Future State of affairs)

> **Especially in terms of careers: You can't get to where you're going if you don't know where you're coming from.**
> *Dahk Knox*

The Future State

Unlike the Present State, your Future State of professional affairs is better defined as, "a personal dream with a built in set of plans and expectations." Like the previous quote said, "You can't get to where you're going if you don't know where you're coming from." You cannot adequately and intelligently define your Future State until you have identified a complete understanding of your Present State and have established a firm basis for making such a change in your life.

Identifying all aspects of your Present State is necessary so you won't go off half cocked and make the same old mistakes again. If you did it would be a travesty, a comedy of errors as is oftentimes said. It would be a real lack of poor planning, or no planning might even be more appropriate. You get to choose!

To make sure you won't repeat certain unproductive, inappropriate or self-defeating behaviors which caused you pain, anxiety and consternation on the job you've just left, or have decided to leave, you must review the following questions and achieve personal clarity. After you answer those questions, do your best to ascertain or root out the reasons for your answers. Remember, you don't want to repeat your past performance, nor do you want to continue working for or under the same conditions which just forced you out of a job/career. You are looking for "better."

Below are the questions you need to answer via very personal and objective assessment to the best of your ability. You may find it necessary to engage the services of a professional guidance counselor to help you dissect you responses and make sense of what you've said. You do need a knowledgeable third party objective viewpoint. Don't tackle this by yourself. You owe the success of this step to yourself, so get assistance.

Self-Assessment Of Present Job Or Career Questions

Directions: You should both rate the answers to these questions and write some short responses which describe your feelings and attitudes about what you've been asked.

When rating, use the scale of 10 to 1: with 10 being the highest score and 1 being the lowest score. Any response which is lower than a 7 should be indicative of you strongly considering the possibility of making an occupational/work change. If you have many scores of 7 and below, you should consider changing your job for sure. If your field of work, not your job per se, is your career, then you need to look very closely at seeking professional vocational counseling in order to investigate a new career field.

(1) How much effort do I put forth to do my job?

Numerical Rating:_____

Written Response:_____
_____
_____
_____

(2) What level of work effort do I exude for my tasks?

Numerical Rating:____

Written Response:_____
_____
_____
_____
_____

> **The first essential of doing a job well is the wish to see the job done at all.**
> *Franklin Delano Roosevelt*

(3) How adaptable have I been to my work: the overall duties and responsibilities?

Numerical Rating:_____

Written Response:_____
_____
_____
_____

(4) How much authority do I have to solve problems at work?

Numerical Rating:_____

Written Response:_____
_____
_____
_____

(5) How many opportunities do I have to solve problems at work?

Numerical Rating:_____

Written Response:_____
_____
_____
_____

(6) How much ability do I have to make decisions and solve problems at work?

Numerical Rating:_____

Written Response:_____
_____
_____
_____

**We should live and learn; but by the
time we've learned, it's too late to live.**
Carolyn Wells

(7) How often am I allowed to make important decisions at work?

Numerical Rating:_____

Written Response:_____
_____
_____
_____
_____

> **Tact is changing the subject without changing your mind.**

(8) How much recognition am I given for my hard efforts and extra contributions at work?

Numerical Rating:_____

Written Response:_____
_____
_____
_____
_____

(9) What kind of working relationships have I established with my colleagues at work?

Numerical Rating:_____

Written Response:_____
_____
_____
_____
_____

(10) How do I communicate with others at work?

Numerical Rating:_____

Written Response:_____
_____
_____
_____
_____

> **One of the things I learned the hard way was that it does not pay to get discouraged. Keeping busy and making optimism a way of life can restore your faith in yourself.**
> *Lucille Ball*

(11) Why am I having communication problems with my colleagues at work? (Don't answer if you're not having problems).

Numerical Rating:_____

Written Response:_____
_____
_____
_____

(12) Is my work productivity high or low and good or bad?

Numerical Rating:_____

Written Response:_____
_____
_____
_____

> **Trust your intuition and forget your fears. Think out what you do. Chances are you'll be less apt to remember what's bothering you. By focusing on your goal, without any inhibitions blocking your way, you'll succeed.**
> *Dahk Knox*

(13) Why is my work productivity so poor? (Don't answer this question if your work productivity is good.)

Numerical Rating:_____

Written Response:_____
_____
_____
_____

(14) How self-sufficient am I at work?

Numerical Rating:_____

Written Response:_____
_____
_____
_____

(15) How much job freedom and flexibility do I have?

Numerical Rating:_____

Written Response:_____
_____
_____
_____

(16) How skilled am I at my job?

Numerical Rating:_____

Written Response:_____
_____
_____
_____
_____

(17) How well do I manage and lead others?

Numerical Rating:_____

Written Response:_____
_____
_____
_____

Advice: Wise men don't need it, fools don't heed it.

---

(18) How much progressive growth opportunity and training development is offered or made available to me at work?

Numerical Rating:_____ (Rate this to the degree you take advantage of it)

Written Response:_____
_____
_____
_____
_____

(19) How does my position salary match up with similar position salaries at other competitive companies?

Numerical Rating:_____

Written Response:_____
_____
_____
_____
_____

> **The world seems to be changing so fast nowadays you couldn't stay wrong all the time even if you tried.**
> Bits & Pieces 5/90

> **Start today by uncluttering your mind and thinking simply and clearly. Vision needs room to focus.**
> Dahk Knox

(20) How much advancement/promotion opportunity exists in my job?

Numerical Rating:_____

Written Response:_____
_____
_____
_____
_____

(21) What are my summarized feelings about my present position?

Your Objective Response:_____
_____
_____
_____
_____
_____
_____

The young make the mistake of thinking that education can take the place of experience; the old, that experience place of education.
Bits & Pieces, 5/90

Idealizing Your Future State Of Affairs

Assuming you've finished with the Present State questions, and you have all of your ducks in a row, "quack, quack," not you, the ducks, then you should proceed with defining your Future State. That is, how you idealize your Future State. What should it look like? Deal with the nitty gritty of the dream and develop for yourself the world you'd be most happy in: your new career field. Paint yourself a picture of your ideal Future State.

The glitter of a new home and better vehicles and sparkling diamonds and gold jewelry is for later. Much later. The picture you're most concerned with here is your job, your occupation, your new vocation, your career of the future. So start defining the way you'd like it to look. Example to follow.

Needless to say, the job the authors will illustrate is only one example from thousands of possibilities. You'll have to be the ultimate designer and planner of your own occupation, a vocational counselor is only your hired consultant or contractor. *You are the architect of your dreams, so carefully plan each step of the way.* You are also the visionary, the person who gives your dream career dimension and appeal. *So you can expect to get out of this dream career, exactly what you put into it.*

Example Of Future State Career: Let's assume you're now engaged in the health services or the social services industry. You've been doing the same job for almost 15 years and you're bored. And that's just for "beginners." There's no way your company is going to promote you, you've already "maxed out" on the advancement ladder and the challenge of the position died long ago. Even that college degree is no longer useful in your job; it's either outdated or not enough. Your boss gets on your nerves and so do many of the other employees, some who are good friends of yours. You've already noted it's time to move on and you've made the decision to seek vocational counseling.

Having gone through phase one, defining and answering the questions of the Present State, you're now expected to create something, not out of nothing, but something from all the information you've gathered and gleaned during your counseling sessions, and from independent study and investigation. You're rich in data . . . so rich that at one point during your counseling, you had to begin to limit your new career possibilities. Some of that was done through trial and error, testing the waters of business and industry and by making influential contacts with people who laid out the facts for you, concerning a career change. You're starting to feel real good about yourself and you like what you're experiencing. It's new and exciting; it's similar to beginning a new romance with the perfect mate, but not quite. However, you're very perceptive and know the difference.

Finally, you've narrowed the margin; there are only two potential careers left that you're still "gung-ho" over. One is teaching your skill areas at the collegiate level, and the other is to become a private consultant and trainer. Once again using your past skills and knowledge to freelance in the marketplace. The decision has been difficult, but you've decided to go with the teaching idea. Being a private consultant and trainer wasn't quite as attractive as being a teacher for you. Hope you agreed.

The biggest problem has now been overcome; you've chosen a career and chosen wisely. You've based your decisions on data and information you've gleaned through personal investigations, research and counseling. In the end, you've chosen a career which meets all the elements that are most important to you. The final result is a career in teaching. So what is next?

You've come to the conclusion that teaching will be your new career. At this point, you've also considered what subject areas you'd like to study and become proficient in as a "well versed guru" of whatever. You've probably had some thoughts about where you'd like to live and teach, and at what particular educational level. All such thinking is part of the Future State visioning process. Little by little each new piece of information will come to you and you'll fit it into your success puzzle.

In order to fully develop your Future State of affairs, you must give yourself time. You can have a superficial vision or picture of what that Future State will or should look like, but to achieve it, you'll have to contribute significantly to the next step, the Transitional State. The most difficult step is making the transition from the Present State to the Future State. That's where the bulk of your work is going to be. Are you ready for the Transitional State (process)?

The Transitional State

We just mentioned above, your biggest problem has been solved. You chose to go into the teaching profession. From here on out, your planning will be guided by making decisions which have also been well thought out. With detailed preparation and more hard work and effort, you'll reap the benefits of your planning according to the schedule of actions you've set up for yourself. You ask,"What actions?"

Actions Targeted For Results

The first step is to set some specific, reachable goals. Goals which are congruent with your quest of becoming a teacher. Decide what your top five goals are. List them:
Goal One:_____
_____
_____

Goal Two:_____
_____
_____

Goal Three:_____
_____
_____

Goal Four:_____
_____
_____

Goal Five:_____
_____
_____

Those goals may have dealt with such things as *(1)* researching for the best school or college to attend, *(2)* investigating all available financial sources for tuition, *(3)* locating possible places to reside while attending classes and *(4)* achieving family buy-in and support for your decision to return to school, and so forth. The ideas and the goals are yours, you get to choose.

Secondly, you need to recognize the "pro's" and "con's" of each goal you set for yourself. Assess the difficulty of achieving each particular goal and take appropriate steps to deal with complications and obstacles as they occur. Prepare ahead of time and you'll have less of a strain in surmounting rough spots when they eventually arise to inhibit your progress.

So, list some "pro's" and "con's" for each goal. Below is plenty of space in which to do that.

Goal One: The Pro's

(1)_____

_____

(2)_____

_____

(3)_____

_____

Goal One: The Con's

(1)_____

_____

(2)_____

_____

(3)_____

_____

Goal Two: The Pro's

(1)_____

_____

(2)_____
_____

(3)_____
_____

Goal Two: The Con's

(1)_____
_____

(2)_____
_____

(3)_____
_____

Goal Three: The Pro's

(1)_____
_____

(2)_____
_____

(3)_____
_____

Goal Three: The Con's

(1)_____
_____

(2)_____
_____

(3)_____
_____

Goal Four: The Pro's

(1)_____
_____

(2)_____
_____

(3)_____
_____

Goal Four: The Con's

(1)_____
_____

(2)_____
_____

(3)_____

Goal Five: The Pro's

(1)_____

(2)_____

(3)_____

Goal Five: The Con's

(1)_____

(2)_____

(3)_____

> **To get anywhere, strike out for somewhere, or you'll get nowhere.**
> Martha Lupton

Next, you should specify the exact steps you plan on taking toward making your goals become realities. Be sure to fill in the "date blank" provided. If you don't, you probably won't complete even your best intended action which you've carefully identified as being your next thing to do.

> **Live your life each day as you would climb a mountain. An occasional glance toward the summit keeps the goal in mind, but many beautiful scenes are to be observed from each new vantage point. Climb slowly, steadily, enjoying each passing moment. The view from the summit will serve as a fitting climax for the journey.**
> *Harold V. Melchert*

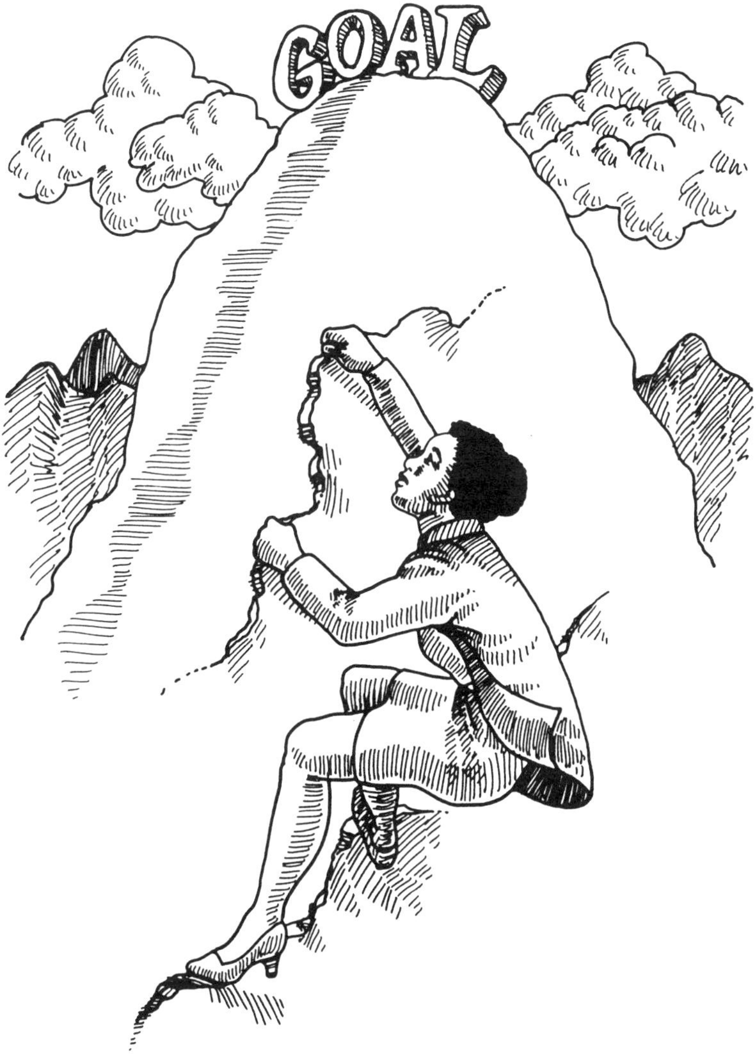
GOAL

NOTES

Action Steps For Goal Achievement

Action Steps For The Completion Of Goal One:

*(1)*_____
_____
_____

Date To Be Done:_____

*(2)*_____
_____
_____

Date To Be Done:_____

*(3)*_____
_____
_____

Date To Be Done:_____

> **Action marks progress. No action equals zero results. The choice to act is all yours.**
> *Jan Knox*

Action Steps For The Completion Of Goal Two:

(1) _____
_____
_____

Date To Be Done: _____

(2) _____
_____
_____

Date To Be Done: _____

(3) _____
_____
_____

Date To Be Done: _____

Action Steps For The Completion Of Goal Three:

(1) _____
_____
_____

Date To Be Done: _____

(2)_____
_____
_____

Date To Be Done:_____

(3)_____
_____
_____

Date To Be Done:_____

Action Steps For The Completion Of Goal Four:

(1)_____
_____
_____

Date To Be Done:_____

(2)_____
_____
_____

Date To Be Done:_____

(3)_____
_____
_____

Date To Be Done:_____

Action Steps For The Completion Of Goal Five:

(1)_____
_____
_____

Date To Be Done:_____

(2)_____
_____
_____

Date To Be Done:_____

(3)_____
_____
_____

Date To Be Done:_____

Special Areas Of Concern

While going through the transitional process, you'll come upon certain personal items needing some clarity or discussion. You may not know how to deal with those items so the next section of this text is devoted to unique elements of your behavior. Those various characteristics which make you the individual who you are. So let's identify some of the possible concerns that may arise and need addressing.

> **Everything we do today is somehow tied to yesterday. Each of our pasts is filled with experiences useful for our futures. To be successful, all we must do is to tap into our reservoir of resources and exercise our innate right to skillfully employ those talents. God gave us that privilege.**
> *Dahk Knox*

List Your Strengths And Weaknesses

My Noted Strengths Are:

*(1)*_____
_____
_____
_____
_____

*(2)*_____
_____
_____
_____
_____

*(3)*_____
_____
_____
_____
_____

There's a big difference between advice and help.

> **We have to have frustrations. You just have to learn how to live with them. Sometimes you win and sometimes you lose, but don't allow yourself to be made a fool of by either success or failure. You have to learn how to rise above both success and failure.**
> *Robert Frost*

My Noted Weaknesses Are:

(1) _____

(2) _____

(3) _____

Oftentimes, many things are very difficult to change in your life. There are also considerations that have to be made for various other specifics, like things you will have to give up. Take the time here to list those items you feel play a significant role in your transitional change that indicate change or self-imposed deprivation.

Things In Your Life That Must Be Changed

(1)_____
_____
_____

Why?_____
_____
_____

(2)_____
_____
_____

Why?_____
_____
_____

(3)_____
_____
_____

Why?_____
_____
_____

(4)_____
_____
_____

Why?_____
_____
_____

(5)_____
_____
_____

Why?_____
_____
_____

(6)_____
_____
_____

Why?_____
_____
_____.

Things You Must Be Willing To Give Up

(1)_____
_____
_____

(2)_____
_____
_____

(3)_____
_____
_____

(4)_____
_____
_____

(5)_____
_____
_____

Nothing comes free, everything has its price and making this career change is no exception. Obviously, there'll be a cost involved for your transitioning from one profession to another. Sometimes that cost is too high and you may be tempted to simply remain in the job you're in and calcify. Look around you, the world is filled with human relics and fossils who have never had the initiative to be proactive in examining and changing their careers. Why? Because they are too comfortable and their false sense of job security blinds them.

How calcified are you? Do you have the gumption or enterprising volition to try something new? Or are you locked into that same old job you've been doing since Hitler was a Corporal? You only live once, so you've got to go for the gusto sooner or later. If you don't, life will pass you right on by. Are you a money hoarder? A person who saves and saves but never uses any of the loot you've acquired? Why?

Listen Bubba, a truck could hit you tomorrow and your life would be over. So what good did it do saving all that money? Oh, we see? It's for your kids! So what fun did you get out of life? What did your life amount to? What did you accomplish? What was your significant contribution to mankind? What kind of a legacy did you leave? What will you be noted for after you've expired? Are you trying to tell us that the only reason you're alive is to work and save money for when you're too old to work, or use the money for fun, because you're too sick or tired to do so?

What's wrong with this picture? You've got to get real Bucko! Start thinking about how you can change your career and still have a good time doing it. And plan on continuing that good time when you start working in your new profession. Or, should we say, "thoroughly enjoying" your new profession? You have so many things you could be doing but you're not? What the authors want to know is why you do that to yourself?

Answers like, "I need the money to pay bills," or "It's the traditional thing to do," or "I have plans *someday* to take that special dream trip to . . . ," or other such reasons, don't really cut it. Those are the type of responses everyone without real vision is prone to make. Tell us, how can you live your life without a "life plan?" Oh, you say you have one? Where is it written down? Go get it out of the drawer and show it to yourself. You can? Oh, you have it in your head and meant to write it down. That's much different, bull! Who are you kidding? You're kidding yourself, Bubba. And if you lie to yourself and do it often enough, that makes you some kind of a loser, a loser who believes his or her own lies. Are you a loser? We didn't think so! What do you think?

The bottom line purpose here is to get you to think about other possibilities and the need for preparation and planning so you can achieve those coveted personal goals. Quit screwing around with yourself and go do something about what you're thinking. Take some action and get somewhere, especially out of the rut you've dug yourself into. My, God! We hope that makes good sense.

If you don't do some careful planning and get a hold on a solid vision you'd like to have of your own future, you'll stay exactly where you are now without any type of significant movement on your part. You'll be the one to blame when you eventually start complaining or regretting how you never did anything truly meaningful with your life, and that day will come if you continue to calcify; after a while you'll become petrified, that's the stage where its definitely too late to change. That's where you have one foot in the grave with the other foot struggling to follow suit. It means you're not looking forward to retirement other than it will end your daily boring grind and perpetual misery. How sad, how tragic a life wasted!

Are you thinking yet? Are you ready to discuss with yourself the costs you'll be incurring if you don't make some career changes or, at the least, will you begin getting active in pursuing some uplifting changes? List below some of the personal costs you'll have in making a transition into teaching. Remember, that was the career we decided on way back when. Then list the personal costs you'll have if you remain calcified and immobile. Notice the difference. We hope its the type of difference that gets you excited, excited enough to do something about really making a change in your professional life.

Good work is often wasted for lack of a little more.

Personal Costs If You Transition

(1) _____
_____
_____
_____
_____

(2) _____
_____
_____
_____
_____

(3) _____
_____
_____
_____
_____

(4) _____
_____
_____
_____
_____

(5)_____

_____

_____

_____

_____

> An optimist is a person who goes to the window every morning and says, "Good morning, God." The pessimist goes to the window every morning and says, "Good God, it's morning!"
> Which person are you?
> How calcified have you become?
> Where is your life going?
> Is it going in the direction you want it to go? No? So, change it!!!
> *Jan Knox*

Personal Costs If You Don't Do Anything

(1)_____

_____

_____

(2)_____

_____

_____

(3)_____
_____
_____

(4)_____
_____
_____

(5)_____
_____
_____

> **Whatever you do, you need courage. Whatever course you decide upon, there is always someone to tell you, you are wrong. There are always difficulties arising which temp you to believe that your critics are right. To map out a course of action and follow it to an end requires some of the same courage which a soldier needs. Peace has its victories, but it takes brave men to win them.**
> *Ralph Waldo Emerson*

Looking Ahead

Let's assume you haven't fully bought into making a career change. Your reason is that you haven't done enough investigation or personal exploration to dig up the facts you need to make a positive decision. In other words, you either haven't made the necessary time, or you're dragging your feet. Either reason sucks, excuses are excuses. However, for the sake of the person who hasn't got his or her act together yet, the authors have provided you with ample space below for writing benefits, which are in your favor, if you do make a career change.

The other possibility is that you use the same space for listing the future benefits of making a career change into teaching. If you recall, our example career was teaching. So you may want to continue in that suit. Test your education, this is one section where educated people usually do very well noting little struggle or perturbation. They more freely find the good in the change.

> **Every piece of marble has a statue in it waiting to be released by someone of sufficient skills to chip away the unnecessary parts.**
> **Just as the sculpture is to marble, so is education to the soul. It releases.**
> **For only the educated are free. . .**
> *Confucius*

My List Of Future Benefits For Making A Career Change

(1)_____

(2)_____

(3)_____

(4)_____

(5)_____

If and when you make the decision to change your career and you contemplate taking our advice, we suggest you carefully examine your thoughts on what you hope to accomplish in the final outcome and make note of what your expectations are. Please take time to thoroughly think through your desires and needs. Then, when you've truly assessed

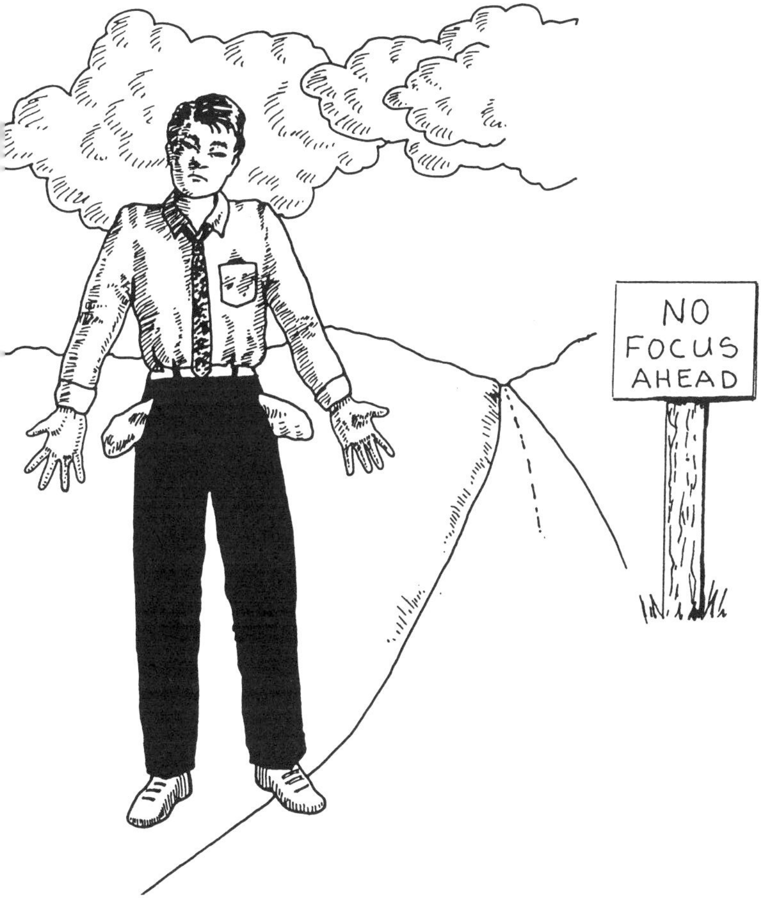
NO
FOCUS
AHEAD

NOTES

all your concerns, fill in the next section which asks you to note the results you expect to be gained from the transition process/career change process.

> **Luck is preparation meeting opportunity.**

Expected End Results

(1) _____
_____
_____
_____
_____

(2) _____
_____
_____
_____
_____

(3) _____
_____
_____
_____
_____

(4)_____
_____
_____
_____
_____

(5)_____
_____
_____
_____
_____

Have old memories but young hopes.

THE PERSONAL PROFILE PLAN

Using The Personal Profile Plan

The following section is presented as a viable method for planning your professional vocational future. Follow the directions carefully. If you use this plan as an ongoing tool, you'll find it is extremely effective. The authors wish you tremendous success in developing your own personal and unique Vocational Career Plan.

How Do I Use The Plan?

This first part if the plan is divided into three parts: your present situation, your future situation and the transitional change. Another way of saying this is, where you are now/ today, where you want to be at some future date and what will it take to get there.

In filling out your present situation, you must carefully define your existing work or vocational status and describe your job or lack of a job and how your life is affected by it. Tell it like it is. Example: I am presently working as a secretary for ABC Company. I make $7.85 an hour, work 40-45 hours a week, get one week of yearly vacation, six sick days and five holidays. I also get medical and dental health care. I live in a one bedroom apartment, own a three year old Chevy Cavalier (paid for), and will complete my A.A. degree after six more general elective courses. I only have approximately $65.00 left each month, after expenses, for recreation or personal luxury use. Now you have a simple picture of where you are, your personal reality.

The second step on this process is to define where you plan on being in "X" amount of time. You must select and stick by the amount of time you finally plan for accomplishing this goal. Never deviate off your selected pathway once it has been chosen and punched into your plan. The only exception for this is sickness or some unexpected emergency or setback. Most such incidents or similar occasions are minor and short term. Therefore, any interference with the plan should be easily rectifiable. Adjust your time process as it needs adjustment due to external inhibitors.

An example of where you want to be in the future is: Four years from today I want to be a paralegal working as a private free-lancer who assists eight or ten small law firms. I want to raise my salary to $15.00 an hour and buy a new red BMW convertible. I want a beeper, a cellular car telephone and a personal fax machine. I want to own my own condo and have completed an A.A. degree and graduated for paralegal school.

Now that you have defined your present situation and your future situation or dream existence, you must begin to contemplate the hardest party of the initial planning steps- the transitional change or what must I do to get to where I want to be?

When focusing on this change process, you absolutely as realistic as possible. This means no guess work or taking chances without planning or provocation. Do your homework, research and checkout toe facts. You obviously will not be able to list all the necessary changes essential in the small space provided for this change in the third step section—transitional change. Starting with the next section, "Tangible Objectives for Plan" through section "Three Key Changes That Will Be Made" is the total transitional process. This is where you plan, item by item, step by step, what it takes to achieve your future goal.

In section "Tangible Objectives For Plan," you must begin laying the groundwork for what you must proactively do to become what you have chosen to become. For the purposes of this process explanation, the authors have chosen the paralegal profession for you. So your first decision in the transitional process is that you have selected to pursue the career of a paralegal. You already made this decision in step two, "What Your Future Would Look Like."

Therefore, one objective you must accomplish would be to select the correct school or college to attend. A second objective would be how to finance this schooling and where

139

to go for such assistance. A third objective may be whatever else you choose. That is, something major that will affect your new career plans—only you will know what that may be. List it here and deal with it.

Once you have selected your major objectives, you must then evaluate the pro's and con's of each objective. This section of the plan is labeled, "Objectives Assessment." You begin by taking your first objective (selecting the correct school or college to attend) and evaluate or assess its good points (by filling in the Pro's blanks) and its poor point (by filling in the Con's blanks). After you have assessed the Pro's and Con's of the first objective you begin to do the same thing for your other objectives.

An example of the Pro's and Con's for objective one, which school or college to attend, would be:

Pro's

(1) Low tuition
(2) Close proximity to home
(3) Less travel time
(4) Good paralegal instructors and curriculum

Con's

(1) Day class hours - no night classes
(2) School parking lot is known for car vandalism; i.e., theft, etc.
(3) Student body is much younger and immature than myself.

The next area of concern is the "Action Steps To Objectives." Going back again to your first objective (the selecting of the correct school or college), decide what proactive steps you will now make to reach your objective. An example would be to start researching various prospective schools for which to apply. Put a date by which this research will be done. If you do not do this, your action step will never be completed. **Never!** You will tend to put this step or any other step off, if you do not decide on a date for action. After you reach your first action step at the appropriate date, go on to your second action step, third and so on. You may need ten action steps or fifteen or sixteen. Only you can determine what your plan requires. Just keep the process clean and simple.

The "Decisions To Be Made" section is concerned with special items or considerations which you may have to eventually face. For example, a decision to be made about deciding which lending institution to use based on loan arrangements for school tuition or which bank has the best interest rates and so forth. So your decision would probably read, "What lending institution should I use, ABC, DEF or XYZ Bank, based on specific individual lending criteria which is." Then you state clearly and list each separate bothersome criterion. This section is truly focused on real hard questions and answers which sooner or later must be solved.

The section on "Probable Solutions To Decisions" caveats on the last section, "Decision To Be Made." You must decide via methods of choice, processes of elimination and/or alternatives of trial and error what answers best fit the decisions that need solutions, real life solutions which you can live with 24 hours a day. These solutions should not be cast in stone or cement but remain flexible enough to be changed when change is evident or warranted. For every "decision to be made," you should have a "probable solution to the decision." Even if your solution is off-base, at least get one halfway decent thought on your paper which begins to answer the decision. A partial answer is a start!

Under the section, "Formal Training Needed," it is essential that you do some outside homework and explore various necessary training options. In most cases, you will find some kind of formal hands-on or classroom instruction will be required. List your findings in this section. If there is not any training required, simply circle "no" and move along with your plan.

Most people do not take into careful consideration when making a life transition that certain unconsidered mental or spiritual aspects of one's life may have an unexpected impact. For example, your religion may not support your decision to work on days of worship or various religious holidays. Perhaps, some aspects of your new career may not align congruently with your goals or objectives. Only you will know how you feel inside and what you are or are not willing to compromise, change or give-up. If your decision continues to bother you, then you should reexamine it and come up with a new alternative suggestion. You will learn these things about yourself as you start thinking about such external or internal influences which do carry weight in your life.

When you consider the mental or spiritual aspect of your decisions, try to derive some sound, conscientious points which truly hit home or have some strong mental impact on your overall plan. Better to learn, discover or face-up to such possibilities now, than later on when you have too much invested to turn back or are forced to compromise when you do not want to. Fill in the "Aspects Of Actions On Personal Life" section with concrete possibilities. For example: You know your spouse will or will not be irritated if you decide to work a position that keeps you away from home for long periods of time. If it will not be a problem, then this is not an area of concern. If it could be a problem, then write down your concerns and the potential ramifications.

Next decide what the "most significant effect" would be if you did make a change which impacted heavily on your life or marital relationship. Consider what would happen if you implemented this significant change. Was your conclusion worth it? Why or why not? Answer these questions before you move on with your plan. You want to solve each set of questions or concerns as you move along or the process will be hampered.

"Self-Assessment of Present Job" is an overview section of where you currently are with your own career. This section will allow you to see yourself as you truly are by looking at your feelings about your existing job. If you are not working, have been laid off or quit your last position, then focus on one of two suggestions. Either do yourself assessment using your last position as a focal point for conjecture and overview or use your presently unemployed status as a proactive job seeker to assist in your identification of personal work traits and/or feelings. Be honest and objective. When in doubt, skip the topic and come back to it later. Remember, do not breeze lightly over this section. It is essential that you come to grips with the realities of what you did or still do on the job.

Find your shortcomings and deficiencies in either of these two positions. Plan to change various habits. If you cannot change them now, plan to change them when you are better able to cope. You may find it helpful to talk with a professional vocational counselor. Testing and counseling on coping recourses may be given. Outside suggestion, direction or guidance may be all you need to help you focus on your weaknesses, determine new pathways for job success or simply find new and better answers. This is not a time to shift blame. You must take ownership for your own predicament and constructively move on toward greener "job" pastures.

In the section, "Areas of Concern," there are two parts: noted strengths and noted weaknesses. This is where you state your own personally recognized strengths and weaknesses or state what you do well and what you do not do well. The weakness are things you can work on to improve your work. The strengths are tools you can use as vehicles to support your career efforts. For example: A strength of organizational ability can be used to help build your personal profile plan and also for job interview preparation.

"Things That Are Too Hard To Change" are always stumbling blocks or silly obstacles you may fret about. You must let go and go around these job/career change inhibitors or you will trip yourself up. State what it is you cannot change and give one good reason why you cannot. Then make a positive choice as to why you will change your mind. Decide the latter reason is worth giving up so you can get on with your plan. Once you have come up with all of your "excuses," and these reasons are "excuses," then you need to positively affirm to yourself and your personal profile plan why these reasons will go away and no longer block you from being successful with your plan. You must want to reach your goals and objectives more badly than you want something painful to block you. Determine your "Why nots" not "Whys" and flush the negative inhibitors down the proverbial drain.

Everybody pays some price for what they want. Why should you expect anything different? You should not. This process does exact a price and that price is grounded in your overall attempt to complete your plan. Only you will know "what you are willing or able to give up." Many times it is money for job satisfaction. Sometimes it is title and power for less stress and pressure. Sometimes it is an advancement because you do not want to move out of town or state. Whatever the choice, it may have a price of authority, power or cost. It may be materialistic or it may be intangible. Whatever it is, it's your decision. Only you can honestly decide its value and worth in your life.

You must also do the same thing for the next section, "Things I Must/Will Change." State the things you are willing to change which interfere in your career change process. Then state why they must be changed. When you have completed this section, go on to "Three Key Changes That Will Be Made." These are the most significant and important changes. Spend the most time on these aspects.

Congratulations! You have arrived at your first view of the "Big Picture," how does it look from the outside in? State the positive facts about "from where" and "how far" you have come with your plan. "Do You Like Being There?" Hopefully your answer will be "yes" and not "no." If you do not like where your plan has placed you or if it does not match with your projected goal, then you should go back and check what went wrong. Verify each step of the process, step-by-step. See where you veered off course or got side-tracked. Perhaps you were not totally truthful or objective with your key decisions or changes.

However, if you do like where you are or will be going with your career change, then complete the last three sections of the plan. Review your future benefits for change, the bottomline personal costs and your expected end result(s). Hopefully, this is where you want to be with your vocational life or career. **God willing, the transitional career change was worth it!**

The Personal Profile Plan: A Vocational Pathway

If you fail to plan, you plan to fail! Decide you are going to work out a career plan for either a successful job change or a transitional vocational change once you have chosen a new line of work. The following "Personal Profile Plan" is a pathway or road map for your successful journey through a career change. If you use it daily and wisely, you will attain the results for which you've projected and carefully planned.

The authors recommend you use this plan when either beginning to make a career change or when starting a new job or profession. Your key to being successful is simply using this profile and sticking to it daily. **Quitters never win and winners never quit!** Besides, it's common, universal knowledge that the harder a battle is fought (working daily on your plan), the sweeter the victory will be (your final realization of a successful outcome, a plan that works). All too often, people start out to change a career with the right thoughts, but on the wrong footing. You must secure for yourself a solid basis for making your desired job change, or career adjustment. It's much better to begin with a proven, workable formula, like this profile provides. Go step by step, slowly and carefully and you'll easily obtain your goals. The profile's purpose is to lessen your agonies; such as, having to draft your own plan from scratch. Use the plan and see how it works. **When you stop using the plan, it likewise will stop working for you**.

The plan takes time to get into, so expect to spend lots of hours developing your profile as you gather information and plug it into its proper place in the outline. After a while, everything you've done and accomplished will begin to take shape and make sense. However, don't expect miracles to happen overnight . . . this takes time and attention. You'll get out of the plan what you put into it, nothing more and nothing less. Please be diligent and determined, it's for your own good. These behaviors will work positively for you as you fill in each page.

Good luck and **STICK WITH IT!**

The Plan: An Outline For Successful Job Change

Define your present situation as it is today:_____
_____
_____
_____
_____
_____

Define your future situation as you'd like it to be:_____
_____
_____
_____
_____
_____

What you'll have to do to properly transition from the present to the future:_____
_____
_____
_____
_____

Three Tangible Objectives/Goals

Goal One: _____
_____
_____

Goal Two: _____
_____
_____

Goal Three: _____
_____
_____

Objectives/Goals Assessment

Goal One: The Pro's

(1)_____
_____

(2)_____
_____

(3)_____
_____

(4)_____

(5)_____

Goal One: The Con's

(1)_____

(2)_____

(3)_____

(4)_____

(5)_____

Goal Two: The Pro's

(1)_____

(2)_____

(3)_____

(4)_____

(5)_____

Goal Two: The Con's

(1)_____

(2)_____

(3)_____

(4)_____

(5)_____

Goal Three: The Pro's

(1)_____

(2)_____

(3)_____

(4)_____

(5)_____

Goal Three: The Con's

(1)_____

(2)_____

(3)_____

(4)_____

(5)_____
_____

Action Steps For The Objectives/Goals

Goal One: First Five Action Steps

(1)_____
_____

By Date:_____

(2)_____
_____

By Date:_____

(3)_____
_____

By Date:_____

(4)_____
_____

By Date:_____

(5)_____
_____

By Date:_____

Goal Two: First Five Action Steps

(1)_____
_____

By Date:_____

(2)_____
_____

By Date:_____

(3)_____
_____

By Date:_____

(4)_____
_____

By Date:_____

5)_____
_____

By Date:_____

Goal Three: First Five Action Steps

(1)_____
_____

By Date:_____

(2)_____
_____

By Date:_____

(3)_____
_____

By Date:_____

(4)_____
_____

By Date:_____

(5)_____
_____

By Date:_____

Key Decisions To Be Made

(1) _____

(2) _____

(3) _____

(4) _____

(5) _____

Probable Solutions To Decisions

(1) _____
_____
_____

(2) _____
_____
_____

(3) _____
_____
_____

(4) _____
_____
_____

(5) _____
_____
_____

Formal Training Or Schooling Needed

Type or Training or Schooling:_____
_____
_____
_____
_____
_____
_____

Type or Training or Schooling:_____
_____
_____
_____
_____
_____
_____
_____

Type or Training or Schooling:_____
_____
_____

_____
_____
_____
_____
_____

Mental And/Or Spiritual Impact Caused By Career/Job Change

Effects of Career Planning Actions on Personal Life:_____
_____
_____
_____
_____
_____
_____
_____
_____

Other Effects:_____
_____
_____
_____
_____
_____
_____
_____

Most Significant Effect:_____

_____
_____
_____
_____
_____
_____
_____

Self-Assessment Of Present Job Or Career

How much/what kind of work effort do I put forth?_____
_____
_____

How adaptable have I been to my work: the overall duties and responsibilities?_____
_____
_____
_____

How much authority do I have to solve problems at work?
_____
_____
_____
_____

How many opportunities do I have to solve problems at work? _____
_____
_____
_____

How much ability do I have to make decisions and solve problems at work? _____
_____
_____
_____

How often am I allowed to make important decisions at work?
_____
_____
_____
_____

How much recognition am I given, for my hard efforts, at work?
_____
_____
_____
_____

What kind of working relationships have I established at work?
_____
_____
_____
_____

How do I communicate with others at work? _____
_____
_____
_____

Why? _____
_____
_____

What is my work productivity like? _____
_____
_____
_____

How self sufficient am I at work? _____
_____
_____
_____

How much job freedom and flexibility do I have?
_____
_____
_____
_____

How skilled am I at my job? _____
_____
_____
_____

How well do I manage and lead others? _____
_____
_____
_____

How much progressive growth opportunity and training development is offered or made available to me at work?
_____
_____
_____

How does my position salary match up with similar position salaries at other companies? _____
_____
_____
_____

How much advancement/promotion opportunity exists in my job? _____
_____
_____
_____

What are my summarized feelings about my present position?
_____
_____
_____
_____

Special Areas Of Concern

My Noted Strengths Are:

(1)_____
_____

(2)_____
_____

(3)_____
_____

(4)_____
_____

(5)_____
_____

My Noted Weaknesses Are:

(1)_____
_____

(2)_____
_____

(3)_____
_____

(4)_____
_____

(5)_____
_____

Things That Are Just Too Hard To Change

(1)_____
_____

Why?_____
_____

(2)_____
_____

Why?_____
_____

(3)_____
_____

Why?_____
_____

(4)_____
_____

Why?_____
_____

(5)_____
_____

Why?_____
_____

What I Am Able And Willing To Give Up

(1)_____
_____

Why?_____
_____

(2)_____
_____

Why?_____
_____

(3)_____
_____

Why?_____
_____

Things I Must And Will Change Without Reservations

(1)_____
_____

Why?_____
_____

(2)_____
_____

Why?_____
_____

(3)_____
_____

Why?_____
_____

(4)_____

_____

Why?_____

_____

What Does It Look Like? (State the real facts)

(1)_____

_____

_____

(2)_____

_____

_____

(3)_____

_____

_____

(4)_____

_____

_____

(5)_____

_____

_____

Do I Like Being Here? **YES** or **NO** Circle "yes" or "no"
Why "yes" or why "no:"

_____
_____
_____
_____
_____
_____

(If "no," start all over again. Do this until you get it right!)

Future Benefits For Change

(1)_____
_____

(2)_____
_____

(3)_____
_____

(4)_____
_____

(5)_____
_____

Bottom Line Personal Costs

(1)_____

_____

(2)_____

_____

(3)_____

_____

(4)_____

_____

(5)_____

_____

(6)_____

_____

(7)_____

_____

(8)_____

_____

Expected End Results

(1)_____
_____
_____
_____
_____

(2)_____
_____
_____
_____
_____

(3)_____
_____
_____
_____
_____

(4)_____
_____
_____
_____
_____

(5)_____
_____
_____
_____
_____

Summary Of Goals /Objectives And Expected Accomplishment Dates

Goal One:_____
_____

Date Accomplished or Still Projected:_____

Wrap-up Overview:_____
_____
_____
_____
_____

Goal Two:_____
_____

Date Accomplished or Still Projected:_____

Wrap-up Overview:_____
_____
_____

_____
_____

Goal Three:_____
_____

Date Accomplished or Still Projected:_____

Wrap-up Overview:_____
_____
_____
_____

Goal Four:_____
_____

Date Accomplished or Still Projected:_____

Wrap-up Overview:_____
_____
_____
_____

Goal Five:_____
_____

Date Accomplished or Still Projected:_____

Wrap-up Overview: _____
_____
_____
_____
_____

Final Expected Results Summary

(1) Did you achieve your desired results? _____
_____
_____
_____

(2) Did you get the job or position for which you had planned?
_____
_____
_____
_____

(3) Did you net the salary you had expected? _____
_____
_____
_____

(4) Are your receiving the job satisfaction you wanted?
_____
_____

(5) Do you still have to change or improve anything?____

(6) Are there any bothersome pieces of unfinished business left?____

Lessons Learned From Your Career/Job Change Process

Think about the valuable lessons you've learned from the career planning exercises you've completed in your Personal Profile Plan. Try to sum them up and retain the results for future use. You never know when you may decide to make another change. This completed profile will provide a sure pathway process which works, and all you have to do is reacquaint yourself with it. If it worked once, it'll work a second time. Why reinvent your planning process all over again?

List the lessons you learned below: (you are looking for your successes and failures, good decisions and bad choices, the opportunities you made used to your advantage and the various mistakes you *will not* want to repeat.)

Lesson One:_____
_____
_____
_____
_____

Lesson Two:_____
_____
_____
_____

Lesson Three:_____
_____
_____
_____
_____

Lesson Four:_____
_____
_____
_____
_____

Lesson Five:_____
_____
_____
_____

New Future Career Goals

You realize, of course, if you stop making goals now, you'll not progress the way you should. You need to continue to move forward and set some new reachable goals which will give you further career guidance and direction. Starting today, list three new goals you hope to achieve in the near future.

Goal One:_____
_____
_____
_____

Goal Two:_____
_____
_____
_____

Goal Three:_____
_____
_____
_____

Congratulations on your successful endeavors! We wish you the best of luck for future career efforts. Continue using this profile plan each time you make a new job transition. You may've already noticed that the plan also works quite effectively for other sorted and guided ventures. Use it whenever and wherever you can.

BIBLIOGRAPHY

Banning, Kent, **How To Change Your Career**. VGM Career Horizons, ISBN: 0-8442-8685-0.

Bard, Ray, **The National Directory Of Corporate Training Programs**. Doubleday, ISBN:0-385-24203-4.

Beatty, Richard H., **The Complete Job Search Book**. John Wiley and Sons, ISBN: 0-471-60250-7.

Blake, Gary, **Creative Careers: Real Jobs In Glamour Fields**. John Wiley and Sons, ISBN: 0-471-81560-8.

Boe, Anne, **Is Your "Net" Working?** John Wiley and Sons. ISBN: 0-471-61547-1.

Bolles, Richard N., **The Three Boxes Of Life**. Ten Speed Press, ISBN: 0-913668-58-3.

Bolles, Richard N., **What Color Is Your Parachute?** Ten Speed Press, ISBN: 0-89815-228-3.

Bolles, Richard N., **How To Create A Picture Of Your Ideal Job Or Next Career**. Ten Speed Press, ISBN: 0-89815-307-7.

Camden, Thomas M., **How To Get A Job In Southern California**. Surrey Books, ISBN: 0-940625-28-8.

Chapman, Jack, **How To Make $1,000 A Minute**. Ten Speed Press, ISBN: 0-89815-191-0

Farr, J. Michael, **America's 50 Fastest Growing Jobs**. JIST Works, Inc., ISBN: 0-042784-61-8.

Gale, Barry and Linda, **Discover What You Are Best At**. Simon and Schuster, ISBN: 0-671-69589-4.

Hyatt, Carole, **Why Smart People Fail**. Simon and Schuster, ISBN: 0-671-61941-1.

JIST Works, Inc., **America's Top 300 Jobs**. ISBN: 0-942784-61-8.

Knox, W.B. and J.E., **The Job Search Manual Volume One: Preparation And Planning**. ICAN Press, ISBN: 0-8059-1804-2.

Knox, W.B. and J.E., **The Job Search Manual Volume Two: After The Interview**. ICAN Press, ISBN: 0-8059-1804-2.

Knox, W.B. and J.E., **The Job Search Manual Volume Three: Practical Concepts In Career Development.** ICAN Press, ISBN: 0-8059-1804-3.

Knox, W.B. and J.E., **The Job Search Manual Volume Four: Forms And Workbook.** ICAN Press, ISBN: 0-8059-1804-4.

Knox, W.B. and J.E., **Get Ready! Get Set! Get Hired!**. ICAN Press, ISBN: 1-881116-09-03

Knox, W. B. and Rice, J., **Rainbow Rider.** ICAN Press, ISBN: 1-881116-16-6.

Levering, Robert, **The 100 Best Companies To Work For In America**. Signet Books, ISBN: 0-451-15954-3.

Myers, James R., **Getting Skilled, Getting Ahead**. Peterson's Guides, ISBN: 0-87866-868-3.

Nivens, Beatryce, **How To Change Careers**. Perigee Books, ISBN: 0-399-51608-5.

Petras, Kathryn and Ross, **Jobs '91**. Prentice-Hall, ISBN: 0-13-511908-1.

Schwartz, Lester, **The Career Finder**. Ballantine Books, ISBN: 0-345-36716-2.

Snelling, Robert, **Jobs! What They Are . . . Where They Are . . . What They Pay!**, Simon and Schuster, ISBN: 0-671-66335-6.

Walters, Dottie, **Speak And Grow Rich**. Prentice-Hall, ISBN: 0-13-825803-1.

Wegman, Robert, **Work In The New Economy**. Jist Works, Inc., ISBN: 0-942784-19-7.

Wright, John W., **The American Almanac Of Jobs And Salaries**. Avon Books, ISBN: 0-380-75898-9.

Yate, John W., **Knock'em Dead**. Bob Adams, Inc., ISBN: 1-55850-907-0.

Order Form

#01 **Get Ready! Get Set! Get Hired!**
Text: $24.95
ISBN: 1-881116-09-3
Workbook: $11.95
ISBN: 1-881116-03-4
*A comprehensive approach
to quickly getting hired.*

#02 **Career Imaging**
Price: $14.95
ISBN 1-881116-08-5
*Powerful planning tools for vocational
success. A "self-help" book that
really works!*

#03 **Common Sense Leadership**
Price: $13.95
ISBN 1-881116-08-5
*How supervisors go beyond being just
managers and lead their people.*

#04 **Upper Leadership Management**
The Transitional Process
Price: $11.95
ISBN 1-881116-11-5
*A process to minimize organizational
disruption during management changeover.*

#05 **Effective Organizational Change**
The Strategic Planning Process
Price: $12.95
ISBN 1-81116-05-0
*A process to bring about change by
exploring the basic tenets of a company.*

#06 **The Knox and Knox Entrpreneurial
Profile Indicator (KK-EPI)**
Price: $9.95 ($182.50 for 25)
ISBN 1-881116-12-3
*Tests designed to identify and measure
your strong and weak areas in becoming
an entrepreneur.*

#07 **Just Like You, I've Been There Too**
A Journey of Hope and Healing
Price: $11.95
ISBN 1-881116-23-9
*A self-help aid written to unload
emotional "baggage" from childhood.*

#08 **Rainbow Rider**
Image Power and How To Achieve It.
Price: $13.95
ISBN 1-881116-16-6
*An interactive approach for
understanding yourself by establishing
a system of personal improvement.*

Order #:	Qty:	Amount $	Order #:	Qty:	Amount $
Order #:	Qty:	Amount $	Order #:	Qty:	Amount $
Order #:	Qty:	Amount $	Order #:	Qty:	Amount $
Order #:	Qty:	Amount $	Order #:	Qty:	Amount $

Mail order form or call 1-800-869-1531

Make check payable to:
ICAN Press Book Publishers
616 Third Avenue
Chula Vista, CA 91910

Sub Total _____

CA Tax (7.75%) _____

Shipping & Handling ($2.50 for the _____
first book $1.00 each additional book)

Total Due _____

Signature: _____

Send To: _____

Address: _____

City/ST/Zip: _____

Phone: _____

<u>Note</u>: Prices as of August 1993. All Prices subject to change without notice.

HF
5381
.C37
K66

1993